In Field Guide to Plugged-In Parenting ...Even If You Were Raised by Wolves, *Terri Fedonczak has taken my life-coaching tools and translated them into a parenting guide. This book would've saved me a lot of hand-wringing as I was raising my own wolf-pups. I would've let go of self-limiting patterns and been free to create a parenting plan based solely on my own family's values—which for us involve Viking helmets, mountain lion tracking, and YouTube video watching.*

– **Martha Beck**, Best Selling Author
and Columnist for O, *The Oprah Magazine*

This book helps us acknowledge and heal from wounds in our childhood, then it beautifully guides us to parent in a much healthier way. Terri Fedonczak doesn't shy away from the tough topics, but she manages to keep the tone light and enlightening at the same time. It's a must-read for any parent!

– **Jill Farmer**, Author of *There's Not Enough Time...
and Other Lies We Tell Ourselves*

Terri puts family values right back where they should be— within our own families. She invites you to take a moment to step out of your family rat race and reflect upon what your values are, and how you want to cultivate and support them within your family. Field Guide to Plugged-In Parenting ...Even If You Were Raised by Wolves *is a solid guide for any parent who is looking to get off the train of how everyone else thinks you should parent, work, care for yourself, and instead access your own inner guidance about the family—and life—you want.*

– **Bridgette Boudreau**, Master Life Coach

Under-nurtured parents, this deeply moving and healing book will help you shift your sense of 'not enough' to a place of abundance and inspiration with your own parenting. Terri Fedonczak's light-hearted approach will help you shake off your past history and make new parenting choices that finally feel right. Plus you'll be flat-out inspired by the many creative coaching tools, mindset shifts, and self-care inspiration to help you along your path.

– **Jenna Avery**, The Writer's Circle

Terri was raised by wolves, but she learned how to change the trajectory of her family through lots of trial and error. For those of you who think it's too late to heal your family-based wounds, I invite you to read Terri's book. Terri has continued to evolve as a parent, as she became more connected with her true essence. Following her passion has become her new family value, and her family has flourished because of that choice. If this is possible for Terri and her family, what is possible for you by reading this book and practicing the tools contained within it?

– **Koren Motekaitis**, life coach and radio talk show host of *How She Really Does It*

FIELD GUIDE TO

Plugged-In Parenting

*...even if you were
raised by wolves*

Terri Fedonczak

Field Guide to Plugged-In Parenting
Even if You Were Raised by Wolves
Terri Fedonczak
Girl Power for Good Publishing

Published by Girl Power for Good Publishing, Valparaiso, Florida
Copyright ©2014 Terri Fedonczak
All rights reserved.

Editor: Darla Bruno, www.darlabruno.com
Copyeditor: Lauren Hidden, www.hiddenhelper.com
Cover and Interior design: Davis Creative, www.daviscreative.com
Photographer: Cassie Olimb, www.olimbphotography.com
Illustrator: Lorenzo Lizana, www.lorenzolizana.carbonmade.com
Indexer: Sheila Ryan, www.ryanindexing.com

Library of Congress Control Number: 2013948735
ISBN: 978-0-9898886-0-8

Quantity discounts are available on bulk purchases of this book for educational, gift purposes, or as premiums for increasing magazine subscriptions or renewals. Special books or book excerpts can also be created to fit specific needs. For information, please contact info@girlpowerforgood.com.

*I want to dedicate this work
to my mom and dad. They made this book
and my amazing life possible, and
I will be forever grateful.*

Table of Contents

Foreword

When Mom asked if we would like to write a foreword for her book, we of course jumped at the chance. Being the eldest (and admittedly the most type-A personality of the four of us), the organization of the foreword fell into my hands. Rally the troops to crank out a couple paragraphs? No problem! However, when it came to the content of the foreword, there was some hesitation. We tried to think of our most "Brady Bunch" relatable stories that would sell our family as the American Dream: a perfectly painted image to convince you that this book provides the tools to raise your kids to become that squeaky-clean teenager found in family movies. However, that's simply not an accurate portrayal of our family. Truth be told, we're all a bunch of weirdos.

Coming to us with nearly 17 years outside of our family, our fondly named "bonus child" was certainly struck by our kooky dynamic. However, she explains how it's these very oddities that she treasures the most:

> Normalcy is not often found in our household. In fact the word "normal" is frequently muttered sarcastically by various members of the family, as we go about our day. This may happen when we come home to find our fat, snarky black cat lounging carelessly on the kitchen countertop, or the fact that dinner is often made to the off-key harmony of a Destiny's Child hit, or that whenever a button comes

loose, we bring it into our stoic, often intimidating, father who places his glasses delicately on his nose and examines the garment between his callused, basketball sized hands. Each of my family members is so abnormal that it usually takes me about two minutes to get through a description when telling others about them and their distinctive personalities; this even includes our pets. This is how I know they are mine though, because instead of "my older sister" it's "Kinsey, who's super quick and witty and will guaranteed make you laugh at every inappropriate moment by doing the most inappropriate things" and instead of just having a dog it's "oh my gosh, Monty, he's a golden retriever-poodle mix, which really just means that his fur is made of curly cotton balls and his heart is made of gold—but man is he dumb, like ate through a wall dumb". How lucky am I that when someone asks me about my family, instead of the generic response, my thoughts are filled with all the strangely beautiful reasons as to why I love them.

I joined my weird family in a weird way; my parents took me in without hesitation, weeks before my 17th birthday. To many this seems strange, mainly because it is. I always get sideways looks from people as I tell them I have a sister the same age as me and up walks my curvy, red-haired sister who looks not even the slightest bit like me. But I was meant to be a part of this family all along; I know this because they truly are my home and have allowed me to become the woman I was always supposed to be.

I have been emphasizing our abnormality, because I think our individual success as students, as workers, as friends and as people is because our mother does not parent us in a cookie cutter way. Instead she embraces and encourages us to be who we are as individuals. My mom is the source of the weirdness; she radiates it, and the rest of us are simply her planets. Because of this, she gives us girls the confidence to be and grow into the best people we can. She gives us what many are lacking in their lives to be truly content…unconditional love. We, the whole strange bunch, are enough for her, and knowing you are loved by someone for exactly who you are is the most powerful motivator.

With all my love,

Katelyn, the bonus child

Coming as an outsider, our "bonus child" gave us all perspective on what made our family work. Sure, we've had our share of rough times—with parts of our teenage years as dramatic and over-the-top as scenes in soap operas. Yet, instead of our screams being matched or ignored, our mom consistently implemented discipline without anger or disrespect. We can all recall stories where our problem felt more important than anything else in the world; we felt that if we didn't get what we wanted, the world would come to an end. No matter how loud we screamed or how many different ways we told our mom how unfair she was (or whatever various stinging epithets we could come up with) our anger was never reflected. Instead, she would constantly reiterate how much we were loved, and that once we felt like talking she would be there. Once the teenage hormones cooled and the anger subsided, lo and behold her point of view was usually right, and she would be right there waiting for us with a hug.

Still in the thick of her teenage years, certainly with a few more battles ahead, my youngest sister, Emily, already appreciates the techniques utilized by our mother during our soap-opera-like dramas:

There is so much to say about having Terri Fedonczak as a mom. She's absolutely wacky, caring, a great role model, and above all, a great friend. She values respect for yourself and other people, being kind toward others, and doing it all with a wicked sense of humor. So, if she's all of these things + a great mom, why shouldn't you trust her? These techniques have been working for 22 years and still haven't failed. Also, they shaped awesome kids (well at least one awesome kid)! One of the techniques that worked the best for me, also that I still laugh at looking back today, is her use of consistent discipline without anger. She put this technique into play when a stubborn little four-year-old (me) would not wear a coat outside. I said, "Mommy, no!" and she replied with, "Emily who's gonna' win when we argue?" To that I mumbled, "You are." She then put a huge mommy smile on her face and said, "Then why do we fight? Let's stop fighting and go get a lollipop!" She used this technique with me on multiple occasions. And as much as it scares me thinking about the future, I know that I will use these techniques, especially the one previously mentioned, on my kids. She has made me into the driven, ambitious kid that I am today.

So, thank you Mom for being......AWESOME!

Emily,

The volleyball princess

Even through the times that we wanted to hate her the most, her genuine love and care for us overpowered our negative feelings. This deep-rooted enthusiasm and concern makes itself apparent in all aspects of her life. When reflecting upon her values as a mother, it was precisely this aspect that stuck out most for my middle sister:

When Katelyn suggested that we help write the foreword to Mom's book, I thought it was a great idea. After reading Katelyn's passage, I couldn't think of a better way to describe our family than exactly what she said. She perfectly encompassed how each of us feels and our own quirks that somehow make our family work. But I still needed to write my passage. My lame first attempt didn't satisfy my mom. In fact, as of today, I'm pretty sure she has asked me roughly seventeen times if I really felt like my passage was a good representation of *me*.

And that's kind of how it goes with my mom. She doesn't ask how you're feeling today; instead she asks if you're showing up in your life today. She doesn't offer to buy you ice cream when you're overwhelmed, but asks you if you've meditated lately. It wasn't always like this. I remember the days when Mom would come home right before dinner from her real estate job, and the air seemed to buzz with tension. It was just understood that you didn't question Mom when she first came home; she had to decompress first.

All of our lives changed after Mom got breast cancer. At the time, I was considered medically obese, hated myself, and had almost no self-confidence. I didn't deal with my mom's cancer openly. I'd cry in my car before I stepped into my house, and I'd hide food in my car, so that my eating wasn't another thing my mom had to worry about. After her mastectomy, my mom started to change. She stopped going to the office as much and started to hang out around the house more. Slowly, the competition I had felt with my mom for so many years started to subside, and I could see her for herself, rather than someone I was constantly being compared to. Breast cancer forced my mom to change her life to focus on what was most important. I realize that not everyone has a dramatic low point that forces them to embrace the joy in life, but I also know that many people aren't making an effort to find their joy.

If I could describe my mom with one word it would be "passion." Even for the oddest things, like knitting, my mom operates with full-fledged passion. The one thing she approaches with more passion than anything else is her children: from Emily, who can hold her own in a battle of sarcasm with her older sisters, who are at least six years her senior, to Katelyn who is quiet and stubborn with a nice combination of sweetness. Then there's Kinsey who is the true representation of attitude and success. And last but not least there's me, the self-proclaimed black sheep of the family, goofy and weird as the day is long. My mom approaches each of us with a desire for us to pursue our passions with as much ferocity as she pursues her own. Despite how different and weird our family is, as we sit around the dinner table mimicking each other and giving wet willies, we work because of my mom's passion and love. I can't fully put into words why you should trust my mom's advice, because I can't fully put into words the love and passion she has taught us, or the difference this has made in my life. But what I do know is that no matter where I am in life, or what I'm doing, my mom will be a constant source of inspiration of how to live life with passion and joy. And that's something I wouldn't trade for the world.

Alyssa,

The Middle Child and former broken-wing-repair person

We see ourselves, each of us with our quirks and different, yet equally strong, personalities, and we see that our mom serves as the glue that holds us all together. If there is one, single message we could impart to you about her and her parenting style, it would simply be "love." Approach all things and people with unconditional love. This feeling of acceptance and understanding, an appreciation of who we are (no matter how odd), is something we have all been given by our mother. She has instilled in each of us a solid sense of confidence and self-worth that no one will be able to take away. For that, we will be forever grateful.

Kinsey

The Golden Child

Acknowledgments

First I want to thank my editor, Darla Bruno. When I first hired her, this manuscript was a sixty-page glorified brochure of disconnected thoughts on parenting. She told me that she would be happy to edit it the way it was, but it wanted to be more. That started a journey of eighteen months of edits and re-writes to arrive at the work you now hold in your hands. I started to believe in myself, and my work, because Darla believed in me.

Next, I want to thank my family, David, Kinsey, Alyssa, Katelyn, and Emily. You all make parenting fun! Whether it's Christmas crafts or witty repartee in faraway lands, you guys give my life meaning. Thank you, Kinsey, for making me look so good as a parent; you earn your Golden Child status every day. Thank you, Alyssa, for showing me how to cherish life in a way that is both hilarious and heart breaking, often at the same time. Thank you, Katelyn, for allowing me to be your mom, even for a little while; it is a privilege to watch you grow into a powerful young woman. Thank you, Emily, for showing me what unbridled confidence can accomplish; see, I told you being an only child wouldn't be so bad! Thank you, David, for standing by me and always making me laugh, even when crying seemed like the only option. I'm going to admit it, in print; you are the funny one! I love you all more than you can ever comprehend.

Thank you to Janica Smith for shepherding this book, Cathy and Jack Davis for making it look so pretty, Smith Publicity, Inc.

for releasing me into the world, Sheri Bennefeld for helping me see beyond my imagined limitations, Jill Farmer, Pat Singer, and Dr. Dawn Dalili for always lifting me up or giving me a kick in the butt, whichever was more appropriate, Bridgette Boudreau for your loving guidance, and Martha Beck for giving me the inspiration and the tools to turn my life around.

Finally, thanks to my Pride: Alis, Angie, Beverly, Caitlin, Darci, Donna, Johannah, Judy, Emily, Karen, Kim, Koren, Laurie, Lesley, Lisa, Lizzie, Mary, Maya, Nancy, Natalie, Rachel, Robin, Sarah, Tara, Teresa, Trish, and Vicky. You have supported me by brainstorming, reading, and discussing relationships and parenting in a way that helped me shape this book and my life. Thanks for having my back!

Not That Wolves
Are Bad or Anything...

I want to begin by saying that my parents weren't bad people; they were just bad parents. I have coined the term "wolf babies" to describe people like me who were raised by parents who were basically decent (and some who were far from decent) but didn't have a clue how to nurture and care for a child.

My mother was a beloved member of her community for ninety years, and she spent her life helping the less-fortunate members of our society. She volunteered for a number of charities that benefited women and children and pioneered the Guardian Ad Litem program in our county (court appointed guardians for the rights of children in cases involving child abuse). She was a pistol who raced cars and flew planes at a time when women didn't do such things. My mother never met a rule she didn't want to break, or at least bend. She earned her pilot's license during WWII so she could ferry planes cross-country for the war effort; she told me this was as close as a woman could get to being a fighter pilot at that time. In her divorce from my father in the late 1960s (her first husband had left her a widow with three children in the late 1950s—half-siblings that were much older and out of the house by the time I was in kindergarten), she got custody of me and my parents' auto-racing team. In the late 1960s and early 1970s, she traveled all over the country competing in S.C.C.A (Sports Car Club of America) events. The newspapers called her "The Red-Headed Grandmother."

Since I'm from a small town, and ours was one of the town's founding families, everyone knew my mom. Invariably, the reaction to hearing the identity of my mother was: "Oh my God, I LOVE your mother! She's so (fill in the blank: funny, sassy, kind, brave)!" Whenever anyone told me how amazing my mom was, I would always think, *yeah, well, she's not your mother*! but instead, I would say, "Yep, she's a pip!" Even though I know my mom loved me, she was too much of a party girl to want to stay home and parent me. Since I was raised as an only child, that means I was left alone or with sketchy babysitters…a lot.

As a child, I never felt safe. Since I had no expectation of consistent care, I was always left wanting when it came to nurturing. As a result, I grew up wanting someone to support me, and I sought that support from anyone who looked in my direction. I had a lot of light, but I gave it away to anyone who would give me a bit of comfort. This made my experience in high school, college and beyond one long hunt for a series of broken partners who looked to me to make them whole. In hindsight, participating in these relationships was really an excuse to distract myself with other people's problems, that way I didn't have to deal with my own. As long as I could focus on filling up someone else, I could ignore the fact that filling myself was my only path to joy. I believe this ransoming my energy for attention was a direct result of a childhood filled with emotional neglect from my mother. And then there was the physical part.

My father was even less equipped than my mother to be a parent. He was an abused child who perpetuated the cycle with me. I found out later in life that my mother knew about my father's history of child abuse, both as receiver and perpetrator, and yet she still sent me to visit him after the divorce. I thought that the visits were court mandated, but they weren't. She had sole custody of me and chose to send me to a man with a history of being a sexual predator. She thought it was important for me to have a relationship with my father, and she thought I would be safe, because he was my father…wrong. I also believe that she was so head-over-heels in love with him that she didn't want to lose connection with him after the divorce. And she ransomed me to maintain that connection; maybe not consciously, but that's the choice she made.

I understand her attraction to my charming father. He was a brilliant man who spoke seven languages, an author, a professional boxer, and a soldier (he fought both in the Special Forces and as a mercenary). He could also play the piano and sing Irish drinking songs in a velvety tenor. When he visited us after the divorce, it was a toss-up on whether merriment or death threats against my mother would ensue. In one instance, I remember him pulling a gun on her when she refused to acquiesce to one of his demands; even at the age of four, I knew something was amiss with this situation. It is only now, living in a house filled with love and consistent nurturing, that I can look back and see how bizarre my childhood was, and how it was the perfect place for me to come up with a parenting plan that was very different and uniquely my own.

In the last years of his life, I was my father's guardian. After nearly twenty years of sporadic and mostly threatening contact from him, I received a call just before Christmas 2007 from a man who said that my father had been staying with him for a few weeks; before that, my father had been living in a homeless shelter. As my father and I had no contact at all in the preceding years, this came as a surprise. This angel of mercy said that he was going to visit his daughter for Christmas, and he didn't want to leave my father alone, as his mental capacity was very shaky.

This phone call began a new journey in caretaking for me. Since I was the only product of my parents' union, I was the only one to care for my father in his dementia colored old age. Alzheimer's turned this man I had feared and loathed for years into a feeble shell of his former ferocity. Alzheimer's also allowed me to have a chance to forgive my father. I remember one day, toward the end of his life, my dad and I were walking slowly around the memory care facility, where I would visit him as often as I could. He asked me a question that still chokes me up when I reflect upon it. "Terri, have I been a good father to you? I don't remember, but I don't think I've been a very good father." This shocked me, as my dad had never been one to question his own motives; he was more a "shoot now, ask questions later" kind of guy. As I looked into his rheumy, anxious eyes, I felt something break inside me...it was years of pain and resentment cracking open. So, I squeezed his hand and told him that lately he'd been doing just fine. He gave me a big grin and said, "Oh good; I was worried there for a minute!"

He died about a month later. Right to the very end, whenever I visited, he exclaimed to anyone nearby how beautiful and intelligent I was and how lucky he was to be my father. The administrator of the nursing home said I was the first person she had ever known who was thankful for Alzheimer's. Without that insidious disease, my father and I wouldn't have had the chance to start over, and I may never have learned the power of forgiveness, an act that is vitally important for wolf babies to move on with their lives.

From August of 2010 to August of 2011, I lost my right breast to cancer, my father to a heart attack at age 85, and my mother to cancer at the age of 90. It was a difficult period in my life, yet I gained a valuable perspective that I'm not sure I could have received without so much loss and grief. The diagnosis of breast cancer, the resulting surgery, and about a year of recovery were necessary to drum into my thick head the importance of self-care, not only for myself but for me to teach my children. It took the death of my mother to demonstrate to me how lucky I am to have all the tools in my life-coaching toolbox—beginning with the Change Cycle. When your life throws you into Square One three times in one year, it's comforting to know there's a way out (we talk all about the Change Cycle and Square One in Section Two). And the death of my father taught me that forgiveness is a gift that is better given sooner than later.

Forgiveness is one of the keys to unlock the wolf-baby trap. Until you forgive your parents for whatever they did or didn't do to or for you, you can't build a parenting plan upon a clean slate. You also can't accept yourself just the way you are…warts and all. Acceptance is another key. Until you can forgive the lack of parenting and accept yourself as the parent you are, you cannot start to craft a plan to become the parent you want to be. Even though I had some pretty crummy things happen to me as a kid, I look upon my childhood as a gift; being raised by one parent who really wasn't interested in caretaking has helped me become the parent that I am today. I didn't have a parenting model to follow, so I had to come up with my own. That was a fortunate turn of events for me, as I was free to choose exactly how I wanted to raise my girls without any fear of whether or not I was living up to my parents' standards. I knew the results of parenting the way my parents did, and I wanted a vastly different experience for my children.

After college, I moved to San Diego to attend law school; it only took a semester for me to figure out that I didn't want to be a lawyer. I stayed in San Diego for eight years, and that's where I met and married my was-band (this is one of my favorite terms used by my teacher and inspiration, Martha Beck). In the seven years we were together, we had two beautiful children and one ugly marriage. In 1994, I moved back home to Florida with my then husband of five years, so I could raise my two girls where the air was clear and the public schools were safe. I missed having any support system for child rearing, as we had no family at all in San Diego. At least in Florida I had my mom as part-time babysitter and a job for me in the family business. The result of the move home was an awareness of all that was wrong with my marriage. Between 1994 and 1997, I survived a nasty divorce, met, and then married, my sweet husband of sixteen years. Together we had a third girl, who is now fourteen. At the end of 2010, we became guardians for my middle child's best friend. She came from a home that left her with a lot of wolf-baby tendencies that I immediately recognized from my own experience. In addition to adding another awesome girl to our existing three, I got a chance to try my parenting tools with a child who came from an environment of lack. I discovered that I hadn't just won the genetic lottery of having great kids; a consistent outcome occurred when I applied my parenting plan, regardless of the test subject.

I originally titled this book *The Zen of Parenting*, because parenting, to me, is a spiritual practice. It's spiritual in that it's bigger than the sum of its parts; parenting allows us to become the best version of ourselves through love and nurturing. We can change the world into a more loving place just by loving our kids. Parenting is practice in that we do it every day, like brushing our teeth. You don't have to brush your teeth every day, but you'll be so much happier with your smile if you do. If you make a daily practice of the principles and tools outlined in this book, I hope that you, too, will experience the spirituality of parenting. My own parenting has largely been cobbled together by watching the *Cosby Show* and *Supernanny*, reading parenting magazines, practicing my life-coaching tools, and figuring out what my mother would do in any given situation, and then doing the opposite. I wish I were kidding, but that's how I started. However, when I systemized my parenting plan according to my vision of what kind of adult I wanted my kids to become, I left behind the reactionary parenting that was based solely upon a response to what my mom lacked. I mixed these ingredients with a pinch of passion, a cup of instinct, a pound of humor…and stirred.

As I was pitching this book idea to to my fellow coach, the amazing Martha Atkins, she groaned, "God, not another parenting book!" I think she didn't want me to be lumped into an already saturated genre of dry, instructional books. I agreed, as most parenting books I've read put me to sleep.

"But you don't understand," I told my friend. "I was raised by wolves, so I had to learn how to parent by parenting myself." She perked up and said that she would actually read that book—a book that is grounded in the reality of coming up with a parenting plan when you have no example to follow. She suggested I change the title of my book to reflect that premise. I thanked her and embarked on a whole new journey.

In my experience, parenting is a practice of spreading your love, not only on your children, but also upon yourself in the form of self-care. If you can take care of yourself by slowing down and noticing when you are in need of recharging, then you can plug into the abundant pool of energy that is waiting for you right beneath the surface of your busy life. I practice self-care by engaging in my minimum daily requirements (MDRs) of meditation, writing in my journal, and exercising. Self-care is different for everyone; in Chapter Three, you can learn the way to come up with your own MDRs. If you pattern self-care for your children, they will pattern it for their children, thereby creating a new cycle of parenting built upon abundance instead of lack. As wolf babies, we are very familiar with lack: lack of attention, lack of support, and lack of direction. Abundance is a new concept for many of us. A focus on abundance requires that you give up the hope that some universal Mommy or Daddy will ride in on a white horse and fix your life; you are your own savior, and you can start living in abundance by practicing gratitude for what you have right now. In my house, abundance takes the form of spending time with my children instead of money on them (toys cannot buy security, only time with your kids can), being their rock when teen drama threatens to crush their spirit, giving them so many hugs and kind words that they can't help but feel buoyed, and demonstrating to them an ongoing acceptance and appreciation for my life just the way it is, warts and all. Abundance takes practice and a tuning into your own needs before helping others with theirs (more about this in Chapter Three, as well). If we practice abundance and model it for our children, we can leave behind the wolf-baby cycle forever.

• • •

I believe that everyone has a superpower, and mine is connecting with kids. I remember the day I learned that I was a good parent. I'd begun seeing a marriage counselor with my was-band, and the therapist had become my second mother. She was a large, soft-spoken, hilarious British woman named Dr. Marie Fuller; sadly, she passed away soon after I married my current husband. I still miss her warmth. She gave me the support and love I needed during an ugly divorce that felt like it would break me in two. I was sitting in her office one day, crying…again. I told her I didn't know how I would manage to parent alone. I had no idea what to do with a one-year-old and three-year-old all by myself with no partner, and I didn't want my kids to suffer. Even though my ex had shared custody, I was the primary custodial parent. That translated into single mom with every other weekend off (or more accurately, every other weekend to worry about what was happening at their father's house, as he was infinitely less equipped than I to nurture two little girls). Marie turned to me with her kind eyes and said, "Darling, you are already a great parent. You have parented yourself beautifully. You are kind, loving, and compassionate. Your girls will be just fine."

And she was right. I may not have been able to draw beyond stick figures (I'm always the last one picked in Pictionary), or sing on key, but I can crank out amazing kids. I've always known instinctively what to do; the times I have had trouble in my parenting were when I went against my instincts. In the ensuing years, I have become a Certified Martha Beck Life Coach with a focus on parents and teenagers, but my basic parenting model remains the same: set clear rules of behavior, be consistent in your discipline, and let your kids know that your love will be there when they need it. And, of course, a wacky sense of humor never hurts! After reading this book, you will have the tools to put together your own parenting plan, one that is flexible enough to survive the test of time and teenagers!

Intrinsic in leaving behind the wolf-baby cycle is forgiving your parents for their shortcomings and letting go of the resentment you may have been carrying around for years. Take the needle off the record of how poorly you were treated or how awful your parents were. These stories don't make you any happier or a better parent, regardless of how true they may be. You must leave your old story behind if you want to create a new one for your children.

My passion is helping other wolf-babies build a system of parenting that makes them feel connected to their kids, thereby beginning a new child-rearing cycle of mutual love and respect. I call this new cycle *Plugged-In Parenting*; it's parenting as a spiritual practice, as opposed to something you squeeze in between commercials. Parenting is too important to leave it to chance. I think Jackie Onassis said it best, "If you bungle raising your children, I don't think whatever else you do matters very much."

As you start on this journey with me, know that I've made every mistake I caution against in this book, and that's okay. If

I hadn't made those mistakes, I wouldn't be where I am, and I wouldn't have anything to write about! I will show you how to use life-coaching tools to clean up your own stuff before you try to deal with your child's behavior. This has been the most valuable lesson I've learned from life coaching, both as coach and client.

In Section I, I lay out my philosophy of why parenting is so important, as well as some simple guidelines to follow in order to have a happy home. Section II covers how to deal with crisis and flux in you and your child's lives; I use the Change Cycle tool to show you how to deal with the unexpected by revealing different strategies for different ages. In Section III, I have included information that relates to pre-teen and teen issues. Even if you only have little kids, please read this part; they will be teenagers before you know it. Finally, I give you a basic parenting structure that you can use to make your plan. So, let's get started, shall we?

If you have questions about the book or are interested in coaching, please find me at www.girlpowerforgood.com. You can subscribe to my blog to get a little love note from me every couple of weeks. Also, you can go to www.girlpowerforgood/powertools for links to the tools that I've mentioned in the book.

Until then, Happy Parenting!

XO,

Terri

Basic Building Blocks for Your Parenting Plan

CHAPTER ONE

Plugged-In Parenting

You can find various versions of the term Plugged-In Parenting on the Internet, however, my version refers to a method of parenting that is participatory, not just parent-as-caretaker. For me, this means proactive parenting from a place of connection, with short-term actions aligned with long-term goals. Plugged-In Parenting is the most important key to stopping the wolf-baby cycle of lack and reactive behavior. When you've been raised in an environment with no support or expectation of consistency, you can take that lack of consistency with you for the rest of your life. If you parent from a state of lack, your kids will think that's a normal state of consciousness and replicate it in their own lives. This looks different at different ages, but it shows up as all kinds of "not enough": not pretty enough, not smart enough, not popular enough. These are all symptoms of the disease of lack. However, this is not the way it has to be; you can make a conscious choice to change your lack-based thinking and transform your home environment to one of abundance.

Living from a state of abundance is quiet and calm; you're not constantly comparing what you have to what others have. If something goes wrong, it's not because you lack something…it just went wrong. Without the lack story, you can move forward to correct the mistake without judgment. All it takes is practicing a new habit. Plugged-In Parenting is the first step in developing a habit of abundance. It means that you are not only plugged into your children and their needs, but you're also plugged into the eternal source of energy...love.

As long as you can maintain a connection to universal love, you will live in abundance. When you feel lonely and disconnected, just look into the eyes of your children to connect back to love again. If you can just look at your kids and feel the love that connects you, you can let go of expectations of how things "should be," and just accept how they are. When you are plugged into other people in general, and your children in particular, you are plugged into what makes life worth living... human connection. When you are connected to other people, you fulfill our herd instinct in a way that makes your life, and the lives of those to whom you're connected, more meaningful. There is no quicker way to better your life and the lives of your children than to bring more meaning into your daily existence; it beats more money and thinner thighs hands down, and you can do it on your own terms. You don't need a special degree or permission from a higher authority; you can bring more meaning into your life through your parenting right now.

Parenting can be the most rewarding experience we can have. If you do it right, you will produce little people who will carry on your thoughts, your ideas, and your traditions, while at the same time pursuing their own independent lives. Then your children will produce little people who will carry on your thoughts, your ideas, and your traditions. Being a parent is the only true path to immortality, despite the recent popularity of vampire lore. I'm not going to sugarcoat it for you, though, parenting is tough. It is the toughest job you'll ever have, and if it isn't, you're not all in. Take the amount of energy you think you need and triple it; that's Plugged-In Parenting. This is why self-care is so important to fill your energy stores every day.

Parenting requires stores of patience and stamina that you didn't know you had, and forget about sleeping through the night for the first year...or ten. In fact, just as you regain your nightly sleep, they start driving, and you quit sleeping again until they go to college. No matter how many kids you have, having another person 100 percent dependent on you is often overwhelming, occasionally spiritual in scope, but mostly just tough. It's tough because it brings up all your deepest fears, as well as all the crap you have swept under the rug as a teenager and an adult. If you think you have life figured out, have a kid; all your illusions will come crashing down around you.

Even though I think I'm a great parent and my kids are awesome, whenever I have even a glimmer of know-it-all, my kids say something to bring me back to reality, speedy-quick. The other day I was pontificating about something my middle child said to me. I thought I had really nailed it with a brilliant insight, when she responded, "Thank you, Gandhi." Bye-bye illusions; hello, parenting!

Little sleep and lots of dependence are why it's necessary for parents to have a consistent energy source to fill their well when they're feeling depleted. Only after you figure out how to plug into source energy, and take care of your own needs, can you become a successfully Plugged-In Parent. Everyone has a different definition of source energy; mine is based on an awareness that there is a universal current of love out there. Whether you call it God or Universe, it's a force that's bigger and more powerful than us; the way I connect to that source of love energy is through meditation, my favorite form of well-filling. You must fill your own well before you attempt to help your kids, otherwise you will not truly be there for them. You will, instead, be expecting them to fill your needs. That grasping energy will want them to love you, show you respect, or make your job easier by just doing what you tell them to do *because you said so, dammit*! To become a Plugged-In Parent, you need the ability to step back, notice your own needs, and fill them, before trying to fill the needs of your children. If you are full, your kids will feel it. They will know that you are connecting with them to help them, not to control them to make yourself look more authoritative. A Plugged-In Parent guides the actions of their child without thought to how it makes them look as a parent. This is much easier said than done. It takes an eye toward the long view, while at the same time noticing how today's actions build into that long view.

The first step to connect to the eternal source of energy is to notice how it feels to be connected and disconnected. The connected feeling is warm and fuzzy; life looks rosier, and you can't help but smile. Think of the last time you giggled for no reason and thought to yourself how lucky you are; that's the feeling I'm describing. You can use this general feeling of contentment and well-being for replenishment when things are not going so well. However, if you don't slow down and pay attention, this feeling might pass you by without filling you up. Even though it seems mercurial, you can capture this contented feeling any time you want; just focus on all the things in your life for which you are grateful. In Chapter Six, you will learn how to set your Body Compass, which will allow you to access your body's wisdom in order to guide your life.

The easiest way for me to connect to source is through meditation and/or exercise. That doesn't mean that I exercise and meditate every day, but I do most days. I make it a priority simply because I feel disgruntled and snappy when I don't. When I feel off-kilter, and I begin to search for a reason, I usually find that I haven't had enough quiet time or sweat time that day. And if I'm off-balance because I didn't meditate or exercise that day, I can always use my gratitude list (write down or think of ten things that make me smile) for a shortcut back to love. A practice of gratitude begins with doing nothing (I can hear you gasp, but doing nothing is a good thing, I promise). You can't notice when you need rest unless you are still long enough to assess your energy level. I don't mean that you need an hour of meditation in a lotus position; doing nothing for five minutes is enough time to notice how you're feeling. Begin the five minutes with three deep belly breaths and you'll be able to settle out of your mind and into your body enough to feel what you need. If there's not a reason for the lack feeling, then it could be the inherent wolf-baby lack attack habit (since wolf babies are raised in an environment of lack, it becomes a habit...a sad kind of normal). When I was controlled by lack-based thinking, I would take a small setback and blow it up into something life changing. I would turn my husband's lack of attention to a full garbage can into a lack of respect for me, and my reaction would be way out of proportion. Just sitting still and thinking of all the things in your life for which you are grateful will reset the lack button that is so often the default for wolf babies. My daily practice of gratitude begins when I open my eyes in the morning; the first thing I do when I wake up is think of ten things for which I am grateful.

Let's start your gratitude practice right now. Go ahead and write down ten things that make you smile.

For me right now, they are:

1. Simply Red on the radio.
2. My sweet husband who is driving while I type on my iPad.
3. My wondrous children who make me laugh so hard that tea comes out of my nose.
4. Tea.
5. My wacky Goldendoodle who makes me smile because of his resemblance to a Muppet.
6. Heated car seats (seriously, I would like to find the person who invented heated seats and give them a big ole' hug).
7. My life-coaching tribe.
8. Air conditioning on a summer day.
9. Beautiful boots on any day.
10. My strong, wonderful body that has sustained me through years of no sleep and crazy dieting.

There...now don't you feel better? I do—each and every time I do this.

Another way to plug into gratitude is by taking care of you. I implore you to reschedule your day to include time for yourself in order to be a better parent, a better spouse, and a better employer or employee; it won't be easy, but the mental clarity and physical energy you gain from caring for yourself first will more than make up for the effort. A great book to read about putting self-care at the top of your list is *The Joy Diet* by Martha Beck. This is a wonderful recipe for bringing more joy into your life. Beck's first chapter is titled "Nothing." As I said earlier, the first step to discovering how to plug in is to do nothing…for at least five minutes a day. My other favorite chapter is the last one, called "Feasting" (the bits in the middle are good, too, but I have incorporated the first and last chapters into my daily routine), and it is one of my go-to roadmaps for self-care. The exercises in the Feasting chapter focus on sensory delights. Beck urges you to name a few things that delight each of your senses. Let's give it a try.

First, find a quiet place; lock yourself in the bathroom if necessary (I wish I could say I've never done this to get some peace), then fill in the blanks with the first ideas that pop into your head.

Sights that make me happy

1. _____
2. _____
3. _____
4. _____
5. _____

Tastes that make me happy:

1. _____
2. _____
3. _____
4. _____
5. _____

Sounds that make me happy:

1. _____
2. _____
3. _____
4. _____
5. _____

Things to touch that make me happy:

1. _____
2. _____
3. _____
4. _____
5. _____

Smells that make me happy:

1. _____
2. _____
3. _____
4. _____
5. _____

My top hits are: I love to look at the ocean. I love the taste of a chai tea latte. I love to hear the sound of Alicia Keys. I love to feel a baby or a puppy in my arms.[1] I love to smell the ocean. So, if I take an hour on a lunch break and drive to the beach, playing some Alicia Keys on my iPhone after making myself a chai tea latte

---

1 If babies are your thing, I suggest you investigate agencies that will allow you to volunteer to help with infants. Go to www.volunteerguide.org/hours/service-projects/baby-cuddlers for more ideas.

for the trip, then stop by my local animal shelter or pet store on the way home, I have satisfied my hit list…and all it cost me was an hour and a few gallons of gas. These feasts are a basic form of treating yourself after a long day (or year) of work that has drained you. In order to be a good parent, employee, boss, or teacher, you must refill your energy bank account from time to time.

You can go to my website at www.girlpowerforgood.com/powertools for a free download of my Girl Power Transformer worksheet to help you whittle your TO-DO list down to a manageable size. I use this worksheet every day. It takes about five to ten minutes to fill it out first thing in the morning, but the time and energy it saves on the back end is amazing. My clients rave about how much the worksheet frees their mind from overwhelm. My worksheet separates your list into "things you will absolutely do today" and "things for the Universe to do sometime[2]."

Just today, I woke up with very little energy. I had two meetings that were scheduled to last sixty to ninety minutes each, and I REALLY didn't want to go to either one. Even though I knew I was scheduled to attend the meetings, in my mind I put them on the Universe's list. I set out to help my husband with a project and called to see if I could attend one of the meetings by phone, only to find out it had been cancelled. Twenty minutes later, the organizer of the second meeting called to say they would have to reschedule because of a conflict. The Universe is powerful this way. Once you start taking care of your precious self, things line up to help you!

---

2   My Girl Power Transformer worksheet is an amalgam of the Placemat Process developed by Esther and Jerry Hicks in Ask and It is Given and Caroline Myss' $100 energy deposit concept with a Terri twist..

One of the Martha Beck tools that I use most in my coaching, and in my own life, is called Eagle Vision and Mouse Vision. Eagle Vision is long term. You are soaring above your everyday life to look into the distant future. You use Eagle Vision to see your future goals for yourself and your children. Eagle Vision is incredibly important to your parenting plan. If you don't use Eagle Vision to figure out what you want long term for your kids, you will never get it. It's like the old joke of the two travelers speeding along the highway. The passenger says, "Are we going the right way?" And the driver replies, "I don't know, but we're making great time!" You need Eagle Vision to draw the map of where you want your parenting to lead, or you will be wandering without a destination.

What do you want for your child as an adult? How do you want her to be equipped for her future life? What does that look like? In my case, my Eagle Vision goals for my girls are built around independence and self-efficacy. My girls know that their future happiness and success resides within them; I'm here for support, but I will not live their life for them. They must own their lives and make their own mistakes to become independent adults. They are also in charge of making their own money; they don't think that their future monetary success depends upon me or a husband. They know that this is their responsibility; the "how" of it is up to them to figure out…with guidance from me whenever they ask.

Once you figure out what your Eagle Vision goals are, then you use your Mouse Vision to build a daily practice to make those goals a reality. Mouse Vision is restricted to what's right in front of you… right between your paws. The daily maintenance of discipline, behavior modification, and lots and lots of love and attention are the cornerstones of my Mouse Vision goals for my kids. Also intrinsic in my Mouse Vision is a daily practice of working out my own problems before trying to help my kids. We talk more about taking responsibility for your thoughts in Chapter Five. Mouse Vision goals are ongoing; you may discipline effectively today, but that doesn't mean you're done. You must build a daily, consistent practice of discipline for it to be effective; we talk more about this in Chapters Six and Seven. Discipline for your kids and self-care for yourself are two examples of Mouse Vision goals. Yours will depend upon what it takes to support your Eagle Vision goals.

Plugged-In Parenting involves courage. To change a habit or way of doing anything takes two things: *courage and practice.* If you're unhappy with the relationship you have with your kids, change something. Just because you've been doing things one way for a long time, doesn't mean it's the only way or even the best way; doing things as they've always been done will get you the same results you've always had. Albert Einstein defined insanity as doing the same thing over and over again and expecting different results[3].

I love the story about the new wife who was making her first Easter roast. Her mother came over to help her and walk her through the steps. Her mother told her, "First you cut both ends off the roast." When she asked her mother why she cut the ends off, her mother replied, "Because that's the way my mother taught me to cook a roast; that's the way we've always done it." As the daughter was curious, she asked her grandmother about the preparation method. Her grandmother said that was the way her mother had taught her to prepare the roast, "That's the way we do it." When the daughter asked her great-grandmother why

---

3 www.brainyquote.com/quotes/quotes/a/alberteins133991.html

she cut the ends off the roast, the woman replied, "That's the only way it would fit in my roasting pan." Sometimes parenting is like that. You may do the same thing because that's the way you've always done it, but as your kids grow, they need a different pan. Flexibility is crucial to keeping up with your child's development. This is especially important when your kids become teenagers, but we will talk more about teenagers in Section III.

Plugged-In Parenting is the cornerstone of my parenting plan. If I take the time to plug into love on a daily basis, my parenting and my life are more abundant and joyful. I make a daily practice of self-care by being quiet long enough to assess what I need, then building in at least fifteen minutes a day to sweat and five to fifteen minutes a day to meditate. This is how I maintain that connection to the energy source of love. Then I maintain a daily practice of plugging into my kids by connecting to them where they are, whether that is a place of sadness or happiness. Then, and only then, can I help them further down a successful path. If I'm not plugged into where they are, I could spend all my time and energy pushing them down a path to a destination that doesn't line up with their dreams (been there, suffered through that). Plugged-In Parenting is a dance of support and guidance, and it's different for every parent and child. Even though each parenting relationship is unique, the basic building blocks of a successful parenting plan are similar. The next few chapters lay out what I've found to be most helpful in establishing my own parenting plan. Keep the things that ring true to you and toss what doesn't fit. That way your plan will suit your own values and beliefs and those of your family (otherwise you won't end up using it). The most perfect plan in the world is meaningless if it sits on a shelf collecting dust.

CHAPTER TWO

Quality Time with Your Children

When I first heard this term, I thought it was a cop out. I was a stay-at-home mom with a toddler and a newborn, and I thought it was patently unfair that working moms—who got to go to an office, talk to adults, and take coffee breaks—were praised for spending less time with their kids as long as it was "quality time." I mumbled churlishly, "Sure, quality time is fine, as long as there's enough of it." Then I became a working mom with an office job, and I realized it wasn't quite the party I thought it was. I hated being away from my kids a whole lot more than I hated no adult company all day, the ever-present burp rag on my shoulder, and diaper ointment under my nails. There's no easy answer to this problem of juggling work and time with your kids, and the mom is usually screwed regardless, because it's up to her to figure it out and deal with the consequences of her decision. Now, I realize that I'm generalizing, and there are equal-partner dads out there, like my husband, who are integral to this decision, but it's usually the mom who feels like it's up to her in the end. At least that's what happened to me. So, what is the right answer to the question of "Do I want to be a stay-at-home mom or a working-outside-the-home mom? It depends upon your situation.

There is no magical answer that will make being a parent easy, whether it's full-time or part-time at home, so give up that expectation. If you see families who look perfect and polished on the outside, and you beat yourself up for not being like them, you're not doing yourself or your family any favors. You can't see what's behind their closed doors. I've talked with some of those "perfect" moms, and, trust me, they are just as freaked out as you are. There is hope, however, if you step back from black and white thinking to search for an answer that fits your situation right this minute. It may not be ideal forever, but it will serve your family right now. You're the only one that has your own answers; just make sure you're asking the right questions.

Our brave feminist warriors did not fight tooth and nail for your equal right to work in order for you to go to an office job that you hate while feeling miserable, because you miss your kids. It's up to us as parents to make a choice as to how we spend our time. The question to ask yourself is, "Why am I leaving my kids, or staying home with them, for that matter?" If you adore your career, like I do now, it's imperative that you follow your heart so that you can teach your kids to do the same. Then you can go back home, or out of your office if you work at home, and tell your kid all about it, so that they can see what it looks like to have fulfilling work. If, however, you're leaving your kids in the care of someone else because you are following a lifestyle that looks good on television, all the while feeling dead inside and missing your kids, then you might want to take a look at that. Does that represent *your* family values? In my opinion, the American Dream that is based upon having the bigger house, the newer car, or the next new gadget can be more of a nightmare when it takes time away from family to fulfill it. Family time is crucial to create a space for your kids to feel safe and supported. This is why I work from home now, so that I can be there when my girls get home. I love that post-school, pre-homework time more than anything. We can debrief and talk about what went great and what sucked at school. This family connection time is at the heart of what's most important to me and my family. It's this downtime that makes the hustle and bustle feel less overwhelming.

With the tendency in today's parenting to fill our kids' every minute with activities outside the home, family time and time for imaginative play are rarely put on the schedule. It's all dance class and softball practice with a side of music lessons, which leaves little time to sit around and chat, draw, do a puzzle, or play with finger-paints. Overscheduling can lead to stressed-out kids and fractured families.

When I was an outpatient receiving migraine treatment from the Diamond Headache Clinic in Chicago[4] (an amazing Mecca where all migraine sufferers are treated with kindness and respect, not to mention a boatload of knowledge), I had the good fortune to speak with a host of brilliant doctors. As one of them was a mom, the conversation turned to parenting. This highly competent doctor, who knew all the answers when it came to handling the manifestations of stress in patients, was besieged by stress about her daughter. Her eleven-year-old was not performing in school to her potential, and she was exhausted all the time. There was strife in the family because the child was unhappy. She was back-

---

4 www.diamondheadache.com

talking, acting out, and doing all the things kids do when things are not right with their world.

When the good doctor talked about their family schedule, it was obvious to me that her daughter was juggling too many activities; she was in team sports, band, and dance class. The child was picked up from school by her dad, who took her directly to ballet. From ballet, she went to soccer practice. By the time she got home from soccer practice, she would have some dinner and watch some TV. By this time, she was too tired to do her homework, much less practice her instrument, which led to constant battles with her parents. She would get up early and do her homework before she went to school, inevitably doing a rushed and less-than-thorough job of it. Then she would go to school exhausted and start the cycle all over again.

After the doctor gave me the laundry list of activities in which her daughter was involved, I asked, "Does she enjoy this?"

She replied, "Well, her friends have the same schedule, and she wants to spend time with her friends."

I asked, "How much is she sleeping?"

To which she replied, "Sometimes seven hours or less."

I asked her how many hours were appropriate for a child her daughter's age, and she automatically replied, "Oh at least nine to eleven." Then she stopped talking and started tearing up.

This doctor, who knew so much about keeping strangers healthy, wasn't applying the same standards to her own child. It wasn't because she was a bad mom; on the contrary, she dearly loved her daughter and wanted the best for her. Unfortunately, she had been swayed into this situation by the unfounded belief that, in order for her child to be well-rounded, she must do as many extracurricular activities as possible, or at least as many as her friends were doing. This is a common assumption in families where doing is valued over being; we've become a society of Human Doings.

I strongly believe that the happiness of the American family is threatened by this philosophy. We need to build downtime, time for imaginative play, and time for self-care back into our schedules in order to return to a society where we care about each other… so we can become Human Beings again. I talked more with the doctor and suggested she cut all extra activities until her daughter's grades came up, build in some creative family-time, make sure she had the amount of sleep she needed and, then, if things went well, add back one favorite extracurricular activity. I never spoke to her again, so I'm not sure how it worked out for that family. However, I've seen the results in my own family and the families of my clients. Scheduling downtime brings families closer together. Closer families lead to more content kids.

We all want our children to be well-rounded and fulfilled, but scheduling the snot out of them is not the way to do it. Instead, teach them to focus on things that make them happy. The rule in my house is "pick one thing." My kids can do one extracurricular activity at a time. This accomplishes three things: 1) my kids aren't too tired to do homework, 2) we have family time to chat, play, and connect, and 3) I don't spend my free time behind the wheel of my car, playing chauffeur. Quality time with your children does not involve looking at them only in a rearview mirror. That being said, carpool can be a great time to find out what's going on with your kids and their friends. They forget you're there when you're driving, so they will say things they would never normally talk about with you in the room. When they turn into college students, you may hear things you wish you hadn't!

In addition to scheduling our children half to death, as adults, we sometimes believe that unless we are productive every waking minute, we will never get ahead. Most homes have both parents working, sometimes long after their latchkey kids have arrived home. This is so prevalent in our society that we forget that this was not always the norm. It used to be that one parent stayed home, while the other parent earned enough money to pay the basic bills with enough left over for a family vacation once a year to a place close by. Now we have both parents working to support a lifestyle that our parents wouldn't have dreamed possible…and we pay a price for that. As a society, we have been seduced by the media into believing that we cannot live without that bigger house or that newer car.

When I was a kid, none of my friends' parents had a new car, and nobody had a Mercedes. A Mercedes was for rich people—and I mean the kind of rich people who had full-time staff and vacation homes. Today, everyone expects to have a new car, from the checker at the grocery store to the teller at the bank, and if you're in any kind of management position, you're slacking if you're not driving a Mercedes or a BMW. These expectations set up a base monthly cash flow need so high that it's impossible for one parent to be home with the kids anymore. We are dependent upon two incomes because our basic needs have changed dramatically in the last twenty years. I understand that this is a simplistic view given our current economic situation, and I am the furthest thing from a financial expert. However, look at what we believe is a minimum daily requirement compared to what past generations thought was a baseline, and you can begin to see a pattern...and this pattern has ripples.

Today, we have both parents working increasingly longer hours in order to make the minimum payments on the new cars, the bigger house, and all the other toys that symbolize our rise in status...our "normal" in the eyes of the ad agencies. And who suffers? Families do. I'm not talking about the single mom or dad who has to work one or sometimes two jobs just to put food on the table. These people are saints who rarely get the kudos they deserve. I was a single mom of a one-year-old and a three-year-old for almost two years before I met my husband, and I cried myself to sleep every night. It was the hardest thing I've ever done, and my heart goes out to all those single parents who are living paycheck-to-paycheck.

I am speaking of two-parent families who make the choice for both parents to work full-time so that they can live a lifestyle that, in our parents' generation, would have been only for rich people. This family has the ability to ignore the messages coming from today's media, live in a smaller house, and drive an older car in order to stay at home and spend more time with their family. I am advocating that parents should ignore the dream of bigger and better that the media is selling. Because, no matter how much stuff you acquire, you will never be happy without a stable family life.

What if the new standard of success was to spend time with your kids instead of buying a new car every two years or piles of gizmos at Christmas? How would you schedule your day differently? If the new guideline said that spending time with your kids will get you ahead instead of staying at work, what would change? I believe that the only way to improve ourselves financially as well as emotionally is to raise future citizens who don't base their happiness on the next new toy, thereby requiring a system where you overspend on credit in order to buy contentment. Instead, they would build their joy from Plugged-In Parenting; they would repeat a cycle that was set up by their parents, former wolf babies who had morphed into Super Parents.

Of course, I'm not advocating that you quit your job to stay home with your kids, if it means going on government aid. However, you know that sometimes at work you can choose to go home. Yes, that might mean that you don't get that promotion, but what is a promotion stacked up against being a better parent and turning out happy, confident children? Which one creates a bigger ripple of goodwill in the Universe? I'm advocating a look at your schedule to eke out all the time you can to pursue playful family time. Spend that time in ways that are aligned with your own family values. Whether it's coloring side by side, playing board games, reading together, or having them help you do chores; decide what your values are, what your family mission statement is, and then mold your schedule around that.

For those parents who have no choice but to juggle raising a family and working a full-time job, it is a Herculean struggle to do them both well. Family is a very delicate ball to juggle. I read once that if life is a juggling act, and if you drop the ball of work or social functions, they will bounce back up, but that family ball is made of glass; if you drop it, it will shatter. You know that you can leave work to spend a little more time with your children, because if you were hit by a truck tomorrow, your boss would find someone to do your job. However, your kids only have one mom and/or one dad. You truly are irreplaceable in their eyes.

I'm not saying this to induce more guilt, I'm just suggesting that you step back and look at your schedule like a scientist would… without judgment. Then shift small moments of time in a way that makes you feel joyful. If you're a stay-at-home parent, that may mean trading out sitting time with another stay-at-home mom so that you can take a painting class or go running. If you have a full-time office job, maybe that means taking some PTO time in small increments to go pick up your child early at daycare to go to the park. It's your time; you make the rules. However you choose to spend your time, turn toward joy and away from guilt. Guilt doesn't help you or your family.

I have a perfect example of how guilt can short circuit your parenting. I have a writing workshop coming up next month in Portland that I'm really looking forward to attending. I will be rooming with one of my favorite coach buddies; the facilitator is a creative dynamo, and I know it will catapult the delivery system for my message. As I was booking the plane tickets, I realized that there was no way to get back home Monday morning after the end of the workshop Sunday night. The flights and the time change meant that, even if I flew back on a red-eye, I would still miss my daughter's first morning of high school; that means no breakfast chat, last-minute pep talk, or first-day picture. I have been through a few rotten freshman years, as both a student and a parent, and I wanted to be there at the very beginning to send her off to the scary high school armed with a big Mommy hug. I missed her first day of school a few times in the past due to surgeries, and my guilt was overwhelming. So I decided to cancel my trip. I really wanted to go, but I felt so guilty. However, after doing my own thought work (see Chapter

Five for a how-to), I realized that I had a limiting belief that if I chose to not be there on her first day of school, then I was a bad mother. Well, that's just not true! I already know I'm a great mom. After talking with my husband, who said, "look at it this way: if you go, at least there will only be one of us sobbing in the parking lot after we drop her off," I came up with a plan that didn't involve guilt. I would ask her which option she preferred, with no expectation of outcome, as I really didn't know what was in her head without asking her. When I talked with her, I was clean and guilt free; I was fully prepared to cancel the trip, if that's what she needed from me. I laid out the facts for her and told her that I was really conflicted. She said it was fine that I wasn't there; there wasn't a whole lot I could do anyway. Then I said, "I know, but it's your first day of high school. It's a big deal, and I want to be there for you. Can we Skype the night before to pick out your outfit and before breakfast to talk about how you're feeling?" She smiled, "Yes, Mother." I could feel in my gut that something was wrong, but I didn't jump to conclusions about her reaction being a cover up for the fact that she was disappointed in me. I didn't make her reaction about me; I followed my gut to dig a little deeper. In the absence of a crystal ball, I did the only thing I could do...I asked her what was wrong. She said, "I don't want to go to high school."

This started a great conversation about her aversion to change and what we could do to learn a different way to handle that tendency. I talked with her about the Change Cycle, and how it was normal to be freaked out by Square One (stay tuned for more on the Change Cycle in Section II), but that doesn't mean that you stop moving forward just because you're scared. You feel the fear and then move beyond it. By the end of the discussion, we had a plan that worked for both of us. With scheduled Skype calls the night before and morning of her first day, we felt like a team. As a team, we could handle whatever came up. With this plan in place, I made my reservations for the workshop. I'm not sure this is the perfect decision, but it's the right one for right now. If Emily and I stay connected as my travel date/first day of school approaches, we can handle any new issues that may arise. If I had a) cancelled my trip based on a rule of spending time with my kids at all costs, or b) gone on the trip without talking with her in an agenda-free way, the results would have been very different; they wouldn't have felt as satisfying for either of us. I want to spend time with my kids, but not out of a sense of guilt; I want to spend time with them out of a sense of joy.

Spending time with your kids can be as easy as finding pockets of time in your schedule and shifting them to family time. One way we instill a consistent expectation of family time is around the dinner table. We have dinner together at least five nights a week; weekends tend to be fluid, as teenagers have a habit of wanting to hang with their homies on non-school nights. Every weeknight, whether it's take-out or homemade, we eat dinner together. This is my favorite time of the day. There's usually a dance or a song involved (much to my husband's dismay, sometimes the dances are mine); at the Fedonczak house, you get dinner and a show! We all talk about the way life amused or confused us that day. Then the kids clear the table and clean the kitchen while my hubby and I watch with a deep sense of satisfaction. The girls would say we watch with the evil gleam of sweatshop proprietors in our eyes… to-may-to, to-mah-to.

You can find numerous studies showing that family dinners improve kids' grades, communication skills, and social skills.[5] The dinner doesn't have to be an elaborately prepared meal; it can be sandwiches or pizza. The important part is the face-to-face interaction as a family. Family dinners pattern social skills that your kids will use in their future interactions with teachers and bosses. They are a way of connecting with your kids for an extended period of time on a daily basis. That way you can see changes in behavior that might not be apparent if you don't have that daily connection. You won't be the last to know if something is wrong with your child. That doesn't mean you'll have the right answer to the problem, but you will know that you need to start asking questions.

It's also important to schedule alone time with your spouse. You want to pattern for your kids what a good marriage looks like. I have been guilty of putting the kids perennially first, which is appropriate when they're little. But when your kids are five and older, you need to build back romance time into your relationship. It does two things: 1) your kids see how you're supposed to treat your mate, and 2) they will see that Mommy and Daddy have their own lives. It adds a bit of mystery to the relationship, which is a valued commodity when the teen years come around. Your teen learns that they are not the only game in town; Mom and Dad have their own connection outside of just being parents. They see that you have a choice of how to spend your time; most of the time you choose to spend it with the kids, but not always. They will come to understand that grown-up time is also sacred. This

---

5 Here's one: www.webmd.com/a-to-z-guides/features/family-dinners-are-important

teaches them ebb and flow. If they really need you, you're there. But when you are spending grown-up time, they can practice being independent. After all, our job as parents is to raise independent, caring citizens. When your kids see that you respect your spouse, they will pattern that respect in other relationships. Spending time together is one of our core family values. We have others that flow loosely from the idea that we are all on this planet together, and the more we respect ourselves, and each other, the better our experience will be. Respect is the cornerstone of the Three Rs, the next foundational tenet of my parenting plan.

Introduction to The Three Rs

One of the basic precepts in our house, my basic behavioral guideline, is an adherence to the Three Rs: Respect for Self, Respect for Others, and Responsibility for Your Actions. I didn't come up with this concept. I heard it on the radio when I was in my twenties and thought it crystallized what is most lacking in today's parenting. If you ask my children to tell you about the Three Rs, they might stare at you like a deer in headlights; you see, I've found that respect is a lesson taught best by example. I don't preach the Three Rs as much as live them on a daily basis. In my experience, this transfers knowledge a lot faster than talking to your kids. This is especially true of teenagers, as they perceive talking *to* them as talking *at* them. Since I began my new groove of leading by example, I've been amazed by how easily these lessons are assimilated.

Back before my youngest came along, I was following my parenting plan of setting rules, explaining the rules, and then sticking to them, which was appropriate as my kids were three and five years old. It was when I had two teenagers and a seven-year-old that it became a little shaky. I went for years trying to lecture my children about the implementation of the Three Rs: how important it is to respect yourself enough to follow your own heart, respect others by listening in class and doing what the teacher tells you to do (unless the teacher is wrong, then you come tell Mom that your second grade teacher has serious grammar issues, and we go to the principal together), and then take responsibility for your actions when you mess up. But I wasn't practicing what I preached. I wasn't respecting myself by following my own dreams or practicing self-care on a daily basis; I wasn't respecting my family enough to spend the amount of time with them that we all required; and I was blaming my job for all my stress instead of taking responsibility for my own actions.

I could have adjusted my hours to better line up with my family values, but I put the desire to "get ahead by making more money" before time with my family. After my aforementioned "bad year" altered my life, I saw that I was responsible for the mess I was in… not my job. And I began taking steps to change it. It has taken a couple of years and a lot of refocusing of my time and priorities, but I now put a premium on self-care through exercise, nutrition, and meditation. As a result, my self-respect has increased to the point that I don't need that knee-jerk respect from my kids all the time. Their respect for me has increased, and our relationship is better than it has ever been. Now let's look at how we do the same thing for you! Let's begin with the first R: Respect for Self, because if Mama Ain't Happy, Ain't Nobody Happy (this applies to daddies as well).

CHAPTER THREE

Respect Yourself
(or What Breast Cancer
Taught Me about Self-Care)

Respect for yourself is of prime importance if you want to be a participant in your own life. Unless you start by working on your own self-respect, no amount of effort will make other people respect you: that includes your children. Self-respect is a slippery slope. If you look at the messages we get from the media, it seems that self-respect is tied to financial success. Many Americans think if they work longer and harder to buy a bigger house or a newer car, it will make them more respectable and more complete, when all it really does is give them more stuff. I have known a lot of very wealthy people and few of them are happy. I have also met families who live in tiny little houses and drive ten-year-old cars that are very happy. Why? Because they are not trying to *buy* security and happiness; they have chosen a lifestyle that makes them feel happy and secure. It may not be what you see on TV, but they have self-respect, and they have the respect of their families, which makes them rich beyond measure.

This sounds simple; however, it's difficult to maintain a focus on building a sense of self-respect at home when the rewards at our place of employment are so much easier to achieve. The respect that you can gain at a job through hard work and focus is rarely found at home. Raising a family is like herding cats; just when you think everything is under control, your kid goes through a developmental change, and everything is topsy-turvy again. Even though the hours may by long, there is a plan at work that isn't 100 percent dependent upon you figuring out what comes next. If you work hard and follow the plan at your job, you will succeed; at home…not so much. It's easy to see why it's so tempting to stay at work, where things are structured logically.

I also believe the temptation of working long hours to make more money is different for women than it is for men. For women, this feeling is tied to a sense of empowerment. Women often work longer and harder than their male counterparts in order to gain control over their own destiny, and that control is at the heart of their self-respect. The promotion that for a man means a rise in status translates to more control for a woman. Status is also important for a woman, but not as important to her self-respect as is the sense of control. The race for power and position in the workplace can sometimes blind us to the fact that our true power lies in being an effective parent and raising productive, well-adjusted kids. You know the old saying, "the hand that rocks the cradle rules the world."

Since I was raised in an environment lacking in control and comfort, I hungered for both as an adult. I had the notion that if I could maintain complete control of my environment, I could enforce a level of comfort and safety. When I was younger and my kids were smaller, this need for control presented as a grasping for respect. I felt that I had to control my kids by setting up rigid rules and requiring that my kids follow them to the letter. I ran a tight ship. This rigid adherence to a notion of "respect at all costs" originated from my own feelings of inadequacy. It was only when I started to focus on my own needs first that the feeling of inadequacy began to fade; I looked less to my family for support when I started supporting myself with self-care. As a result, my kids were more relaxed and didn't question my rules, as they were explained with love instead of being shoved down their throats. As I started respecting myself, my kids' respect quotient rose proportionately. You, too, can begin to eliminate your feelings of inadequacy; all it takes is consistency and a focus on the biggest component of self-respect…self-care.

When the doctor gave me the news that the lump in my right breast that I had been worrying over actually *was* malignant and then laid out the probable treatment plan for my cancer, my first thought was, "Oh thank God, I get a chance to lie down for a long time with a really good excuse." Sad, but true. That's how much I had ignored self-care for the last fifteen years of my life. I believe that years of ignoring my body's needs to instead focus on the needs of my mind, and all its supplication to the gods of stress, resulted in my breast cancer diagnosis.

Before breast cancer visited my life, the stress of being in the wrong marriage first and then the wrong job (it was a great income-producing job with lovely people, but it was wrong for me) led to a twenty-year battle with chronic migraine headaches. Even after being married for sixteen years to my sweet husband, staying in that wrong job led to a level of stress that was unmanageable; the resulting migraines eventually stopped my normal life altogether. I couldn't work, and I certainly couldn't parent. I finally stopped fighting my situation and sought help. The final surrender and acceptance that I could not be everything to everyone saved my sanity. Surrender and acceptance are still goals that I strive for every day. One of the foundational tenets of surrender and acceptance is a focus on your body's desires over and above the mind's directives.

In our culture, we dismiss the body's wisdom in lieu of the mind's stories about its own needs. One of the mind's needs is an ancient, DNA-based desire to fit in. This arose in caveman days to keep us inside the group and around the fire, as odds of survival outside the group were nil. In today's society, this desire may present itself as working long hours at a job we hate in order to be seen as successful, or staying in a poisonous relationship to avoid displeasing loved ones. This need for approval from the group leads us to do things that are not always best for us; the struggle between following our heart's desire and pleasing others leads to stress.

When I left my was-band, I took a county-mandated class given to parents who chose to dissolve their marriage. The woman teaching the class was a psychologist specializing in family therapy. She stressed the importance of taking care of yourself so that you can take care of your children. She used the example of when you are on an airplane, the flight attendant will instruct you in the use of the oxygen masks. You've heard this a million times, but I wonder if you've really listened. Now pay attention: when the oxygen masks fall from the overhead compartment, *be sure to secure your own mask before aiding others with theirs.* At first you think, "That's not right. I have to save my children before I save myself." But you *cannot* save your children if you are passed out on the floor. It made a huge impression on me at the time, because I wasn't taking very good care of myself in the mad pursuit of trying to protect my girls from the ugliness of the divorce. I hadn't been eating properly or exercising; essentially, I was running on fumes. I was short with my kids; I had no patience; and I wasn't the mom I wanted to be.

Fast forward five years, and the same pattern repeated itself, with the same person causing the stress, but under different circumstances. The new circumstances included explaining to the girls why their father (my current husband is "Daddy") was going away, and why they could now only visit him in federal prison. I got wrapped up in trying to protect my big girls, while handling the challenges of a toddler and the wrong job; I forgot to put on my own oxygen mask. Except this time, my body was older and even less capable of handling the stress. After I finally sought help from the Diamond Headache Clinic, I started seeing clearly again. I rearranged my priorities to make sure that I was okay before charging in to save my girls from the shrapnel of such a stressful situation.

The lessons I learned in Chicago, as well as every article I've read on stress management, have taught me that exercise and meditation are the most effective one-two punch in relieving the symptoms of stress. In Chapter Five, I will talk about using life coaching tools to handle what I believe is the root cause of stress… the inability to align our thoughts with reality. You may think you need to work longer hours or that you don't have time for rest, but those are just thoughts. The reality of the situation is that self-care is a priority, if you want to stay healthy. Stress will eventually break your body down; it's not an "if," it's a "when."

Whenever anyone says to me, "I don't have time to exercise and meditate," I remind them we are all operating with the same twenty-four hours; it's all in how we prioritize. Everyone has time for self-care; they have to *take* the time from some other activity... like watching TV, talking on the phone, surfing the Internet, Facebooking, or sitting around worrying about not having enough time. If you examine your day, you can find thirty minutes, three to five times a week, to perform preventative maintenance on your body. Self-care has actually led to more time in my day. I can accomplish twice as much in half the time, now that my thoughts aren't chasing each other like a hamster on a wheel.

Stress is not all in your head; it produces chemicals that will break down and age your body if they aren't released. These chemicals are also built into our DNA from caveman days, when we lived by fight, flight, or freeze. Even though we are no longer fighting mastodons, the same chemicals are flowing through our bloodstream. If we don't disperse them through physical activity, they will build up and lead to a whole buffet of ailments: hypertension, high blood pressure, and tension headaches to name a few (or, in my case, migraines and breast cancer). Stress is the only cause I can find for my breast cancer: I have no family history, I'm a health nut with a great diet, and I was diagnosed at the age of forty-seven. What I did have was a constant diet of perfectionism in an imperfect world, otherwise known as *stress*.

I was talking to my daughter the other day about how when she gets stressed at work, she can't think straight. I told her that's what the fight or flight response does. It takes blood from your brain and shoots it to your extremities so that you are prepared to run for it or go to battle; unfortunately, that means you can't think straight. If you can take three deep belly breaths and quiet the response, you can regain the use of your brain (three deep breaths is the easiest way to settle back into your body, no matter the circumstances; I do this all day). If you don't take those three breaths and build exercise and meditation into your day in some form, your body will start breaking down because of the constant barrage of stress hormones.

Every day, we see examples of people conducting themselves under a level of stress that is presented as acceptable. If the pharmaceutical companies' television ads use high stress as a way to sell their next anti-anxiety pill, that doesn't mean that the symptom is the problem; the acceptance of that stress level as normal is the problem. The ads are very seductive. They present a world where the only way to get ahead is to make more money and buy more stuff. If you want to lead this lifestyle on a budget that doesn't support it without forty- to sixty-hour work weeks, as a parent, you're going to be spread way too thin. What does this level of stress lead to, other than the perfect consumer according to the drug companies? You are short with your spouse, you have no time or patience with your children, and you are pretty much ticked off most of your waking hours…at least that's what happened with me. Quite a few pundits out there imply this is all part of the package if you want to be successful. I wholeheartedly disagree. If that's successful, I think we need a new definition.

When I was successful by this definition, I used retail therapy to make myself "happy," except it never worked. I would buy more shoes, bags, and gadgets because I was making a lot of money, and I "deserved" them. But none of that gave me self-respect. Since I didn't have a good foundation of self-respect, I was obsessed with my kids being respectful to me. I didn't realize that this was driving a wedge between me and my children. This grasping for validation from my kids led to even more stress. In life coach training, I finally learned that the best way to avoid this grasping for respect from others is to build it up in yourself. If you're setting a good example for your kids by taking care of yourself first, they too will put self-care on their priority list. I believe our new definition of successful needs to be based on joy:

successful = joyful

That's a standard that can be attained without spending a dollar; all it takes is an awareness of what makes you feel free. Not what you think you *should* feel according to someone else's idea of happy, but what makes *you* feel joyful.

In order to focus on the inner voice that draws your joy blueprint, you have to still all the other voices in your head—the voices that tell you there's not enough time to meditate, exercise, and eat nutritious food. In our life of doing, doing, doing, self-care is at the bottom of our list (if it makes the list at all), and I believe that's the root of all the stress-induced diseases that plague us in an age when we have it so easy physically. According to Stanford University neuroscientist Robert Sapolsky, "If you turn on the stress response chronically for purely psychological reasons, you increase your risk of adult onset diabetes and high blood pressure. If you're chronically shutting down the digestive system, there's a bunch of gastrointestinal disorders you're more at risk for as well."[6]

---

6   www.sciencedaily.com/releases/2007/02/070218134333.htm

Most of us are not under the stress of finding shelter or worrying about where our next meal is coming from, and yet stress-related diseases are at an all-time high. These diseases all have a component that stumps doctors…it almost looks like the body is attacking itself. Look at cancer, fibromyalgia, rheumatoid arthritis, diabetes, heart disease, ulcers, acid reflux, migraines …they all have a mind-body component. Sapolsky relates that "long-term stress also suppresses the immune system, making you more susceptible to infectious diseases, and can even shut down reproduction by causing erectile dysfunction and disrupting menstrual cycles."

If you have any of these diseases, I highly recommend you visit the website of Abigail Steidley, a Martha Beck Master Coach who specializes in the mind-body connection (*www.anamsong.com*). She has some great tools for understanding the root of your stress-related disease, rather than taking a pill to mask the symptoms, as most Western doctors will recommend. I'm also a big fan of my naturopath, Dr. Dawn Dalili (www.dawndalili.com), who has a slightly different, yet equally effective, approach to the mind/body connection. Dr. Dalili's methods have greatly improved my energy level and stress resistance, thereby increasing my joy quotient exponentially. Both of these experts start with a focus on self-care.

Exercise and meditation have allowed me to have the patience to listen to the daily drama of four daughters, as well as give them the necessary feedback to make them feel heard. Without meditation, I couldn't have hoped to stay current and focused when my then thirteen-year-old was giving me the run-down of who was going out with whom (it seems in middle school that "going out" is going from one classroom to the next, because they don't necessarily see each other outside of school. I find this quirky and immensely entertaining), who was mad at whom, and all about the current pressing issues in her life. These things are *important*. They may not seem important to you, but they are everything to your child. It makes a huge difference to your kids to have you involved in their lives. If you are exhausted from stress, you cannot be there for your kids. Plugged-In Parenting is not a spectator sport, and unless you practice self-care on a regular basis, you will not have the energy to plug into your kids' lives.

The good news is that there is an endless supply of energy in the Universe, and it's attached to love and creativity. If you can make a daily practice of doing something you love, preferably something creative using your hands (I'm quite fond of knitting, which I call meditation with accessories as a byproduct), you can build your stores of energy to the point that you will *want* to play with your kids for fun, instead of surfing the Internet. The basic structure of self-care is unique to each individual. My own practice involves sweating four to six times a week: sometimes it's a weight workout with my awesome personal trainer/jewelry designer/BFF Alis Willoughby[7], sometimes it's a yoga class, and sometimes it's a walk outside. I know if I don't break a sweat six times a week, I won't have enough energy to plug into my kids' lives…or my own. Another daily practice is meditation; it can be as little as three deep breaths at every stoplight to a thirty-minute guided meditation from a Yoga-Nidra CD, but I do some form of quiet practice every day. If I miss a day, I feel cranky, brittle, and listless.

My newest form of self-care is creative writing. I never thought I was a creative writer. I could crank out an articulate research

---

7 www.aliswilloughby.com/

paper, but I "didn't have a creative bone in my body"…or so the story went. Morning pages is a tool that is outlined in Julia Cameron's book *The Artist's Way,* a must read for anyone who has a creative bone in their body, and that would be all of us. When I began a daily practice of morning pages (three longhand pages of free writing…just keep the pen moving without thinking about what you're writing), I discovered a creative person living inside my researcher. This has been the single biggest source of energy for me. When I take care of my creative energy by writing daily and immersing myself in different sensory delights, I actually want to plug into my life instead of escape from it. My idea of a vacation used to be lying by the side of a pool with a cabana boy fetching me drinks, because I was so tired all the time. Now we go on vacation to strange and exotic places, and we *move*. Even when my family is tuckered, I'm out prowling for new people to meet and sights to see. This energetic searching is balanced with days of rest; I call them pajama days. I stay in my pajamas and knit or watch movies cuddled up with my youngest and my two dogs. This is what Julia Cameron calls "filling your creative well." It doesn't matter how you fill your well, it just matters that you make well-filling part of your self-care practice.

All of these forms of self-care require that you slow down enough to notice when you need care, and then take an active role in that care. If you wait for someone to care for you or fix you, you will be waiting a long time on the sidelines of your own life. Plugging-in to your own life, your body, and the lives of your kids takes you from a spectator to a participant. It's the difference between clocking in and out at work with nothing to show for your time but a dent in your chair, and actively arranging your day so you can make a difference in your world. By slowing down to notice what's around you, you can make a choice of what step to take next. That next step may be to plug into your creative energy or plug into your kids' lives...just plug in somewhere, and be a participant.

Self-care starts with being quiet and asking your body what it needs. The reason you can't think your way into what's needed next is because self-care resides in the body, not the mind. The mind is a terrible master, because it can be distracted by the next shiny object that comes along...you know, like e-mail or what's happening on *Real Housewives*. Your body doesn't give a fig about e-mail. In fact, think about the last time you opened your e-mail instead of lying down when you were tired. Didn't you feel worse, more exhausted and depleted, when you ignored your body's signals to rest and instead focused on your mind's urgings to keep up? Only your body knows what you truly need in order to take the next step on the path to your right life. Sometimes ALL your body needs is peace and quiet, but you will never know until you ask.

Start small with your self-care changes. Begin with a quiet practice and then add in the feasts from Chapter One. If you're starting from scratch, try weekly sessions; spend five to fifteen minutes in quiet reflection (I talk more about tips for getting quiet in Chapter Eight), and take five to fifteen minutes to feast on something from your five senses list. This will begin filling your well. After establishing a quiet and feasting practice a couple of times a week, I highly recommend adding in a little sweat time. Again, start small; consistency is more important than intensity. Maybe you walk up a flight of stairs instead of taking the elevator; maybe you park your car at the edge of the parking lot...every little bit counts. Small steps are the only way to effectively change behavior. We will talk more about using small steps to your advantage in Chapter Twelve. When you've put enough small steps together to form a daily or weekly practice, you will begin to see a difference in your outlook and energy level, which will help you sustain the habit. Exercise is a self-fulfilling prophecy; the more you move, the more you want to move. I turned my once or twice a week meditation/feasting/exercise into an almost daily affair. I like to move so much that I bought a treadmill work station, so I can connect with my clients, write, and attend to e-mails while walking at one mile per hour. It builds strength and reduces my lower back problems like nothing else I've tried. But it all started with the small little steps of five minutes here and there.

Breast cancer was a huge wake-up call for me. I would love it if reading this book caused you to re-think self-care as a priority, *before* you get some debilitating disease. Even though you don't think you have a choice, and that you have to work long hours doing something you hate, that's just not true. At least it hasn't been true for me or my clients. However, if it was a choice of losing my right breast or having to stay in my old life of stress for breakfast, lunch, and dinner, then I would rush to the surgeon all over again. Looking back, I had opportunities to change my life long before cancer; I just didn't think I could. There's the operative word, "think." We think we can't change our destiny, because of our boss, friends, or family. These are all thoughts; they aren't reality. If you are in a situation that puts your body in a daily state of siege, you *can* change your life, before your body changes it for you. It may take a fresh perspective and some schedule juggling to allow time for exercise and quiet time, but you can do it.

If you establish a regular practice of self-care, you will be filling your self-respect bank account with every action, or inaction, as the case may be. You will also be patterning what that looks like for your kids. Kids soak up everything you pattern for them. They don't necessarily do what you say, but they sure as heck will do what you do. If you embark on a practice of putting your own needs first, your kids will do the same. The lure of the next shiny object will pale next to discovering what makes them feel joyful. Now that you have the bare bones to build your own self-respect kit, let's look at the second R…*Respect for Others*.

CHAPTER FOUR

Respect for Others

Respect for others is a hot topic in our household. It stems from the idea that we are all in this together…this thing called life. No one has a special pass; we are all figuring it out as we go along. No matter how big your bank account or how many degrees are on your wall, you are just a member of the human race…like everybody else. I remember when I was in my twenties, working at Nordstrom in San Diego, this point was brought home by the customer-service training staff. They told us that it didn't matter what people were wearing or how they talked, everyone at Nordstrom was treated the same…like a V.I.P. They drilled into our heads the fact that you can never tell how much money a person has or how much they will spend just by looking at them. After working there for a few months, I found that it didn't matter anyway. My daily sales fluctuated not because of how many diamonds my clients wore, but how I treated them. If I just focused on making their day a little more beautiful, giving them a respite in the middle of their to-do list and, most importantly, listening to their stories, then I made connections, not just sales. And for me, that has been a lifelong goal…to further connection. It makes sense not only in business, but in life. The old adage, "it's not *what* you know, it's *who* you know" is truer in today's technologically-connected society than it's ever been. The more you can demonstrate this for your children, by treating everyone as if they were a V.I.P., the more your kids will parrot that behavior, thereby creating a little bubble of goodwill that will be ever-expanding.

Teaching your children respect starts when they're little, or the results can be disastrous. I see kids all the time who treat their parents like servants. I don't blame the kids; it's the parents' job to curtail that behavior. In our house it started very early with "yes, please," and "no, thank you." I made my kids repeat these phrases back to me from the time they were old enough to talk. I still say it to everyone, and if my kids say only, "yes" or, God forbid, "yeah" (which sounds so dismissive), then I will respond with, "yes, please?" Immediately they will correct themselves, even my college-aged kids. It's a small thing, but big shifts come from small actions. Whenever my girls invite someone over, especially when they were little, they tell them the rules of the house when it comes to respect. Some kids follow right along; when they leave, they are "please-ing" and "thank you-ing" all over the place, much to the delight of their startled parents. I'm not in charge of what happens in their home, but I hope there is some carryover. If they don't get with the program after a couple of visits, they are not invited back.

I remember when my eldest was in third grade, she had a new girl ride home on the bus with her from school. I saw them walking down the driveway, so I went to unlock the front door. They were standing on the sidewalk, and Kinsey was obviously explaining the rules to the new kid. I know this, because as they approached, and I opened the door, the new girl said, "Hello, Mrs. Fedonczak.

How are you, ma'am?" then she looked to Kinsey for approval. Kinsey smiled encouragingly, and the play date commenced.

In the South, we use "yes, ma'am" and "no, sir" as a sign of respect. I apply those phrases quite liberally with great success, and I instruct my children to do the same. I say "yes, sir" or "no ma'am" to everyone from the sanitation engineer who picks up my refuse to the person in charge of hiring me for my next speaking engagement. This demonstration of respect will achieve amazing results. People smile and want to help you when you show them respect; it starts a wave of goodwill that is contagious. I also teach my kids to listen to people instead of rushing past them. Everyone has a story to tell and, if you listen, you will be considered a friend. Everyone wants to help their friends. This kind of help manifests in many ways.

For instance, I am the Queen of the Free Upgrade, and it happens because I listen. My family has dubbed my negotiating aplomb, the "Terri Thing." It used to be a joke; if we had something go awry with reservations or plans, someone would say, "Mom, go do your Terri Thing." And after a few stories and special moments with the person in charge, everything would just magically fall into place. It's not magic; it's connection. The main ingredient in connection is respect for the other person's gifts.

I believe that everyone has a gift...a super power. It's that gift that makes them an artist in whatever field they practice. I have been spellbound at a Waffle House watching a window washer practice his art. He cleaned the whole window perfectly without lifting his squeegee from the glass. As I was leaving, I thanked him for being an artist and practicing his art where I could enjoy it. He was a little rattled by the attention, but he was smiling as I walked away. I've had nurses aplenty during my many trips to the hospital for myself and relatives, but certain people raise nursing to an art form. I met Sarah on the cancer floor of our local hospital while visiting my mother-in-law. Sarah used to be a hospice nurse, and then she transferred to hospital duty. As we saw that my mother-in-law was not going to improve, it was Sarah who kept us sane. Even in the worst of circumstances, watching her attend to my mother-in-law (as she slowly slipped away from this world) was a privilege. Artists are everywhere. If you seek out the artist in others and teach your children to do the same, a dance of mutual respect will ensue...and that dance will make the world a better place, one step at a time.

I remember the first time I put this love of connection into words; it was in a journal entry when I was going through my divorce. My kids were eighteen months and three-and-a-half, and I was planning how to raise them without a husband in the picture. My first thought was that I wanted to teach them to seek out the undercurrent of love that is beneath the surface of all human connection. For me, respect for others is grounded in this universal love. I recently discovered that connecting to this pool of love is not only good for relationships, but it will also improve your health. Barbara L. Fredrickson, Ph.D. has written an amazing book called *Love 2.0: How Our Supreme Emotion Affects Everything We Feel, Think, Do, and Become* that delineates the science behind connection. Fredrickson notes that "love is the essential nutrient that your cells crave: true positivity-charged connection with other living beings.[8]" Love is what you're seeking when you have an itch

---

8 *Love 2.0: How Our Supreme Emotion Affects Everything We Feel, Think, Do, and Become*: Page 4, Kindle edition

that you try to scratch with new toys, surfing the internet, or other distractions. Dr. Fredrickson relates how science has determined that love can improve the quality of your life and your health, and the delivery system is something she calls *positivity resonance*. Her definition of positivity resonance is:

the momentary upwelling of three tightly interwoven events: first, a sharing of one or more positive emotions between you and another; second, a synchrony between your and the other person's biochemistry and behaviors; and third, a reflected motive to invest in each other's well-being that brings mutual care.[9]

This exchange of love can start with your loved ones, but don't stop there; the power of positivity connection is that it can be shared with anyone. In fact, the more you pay attention to your interactions with strangers, the more joy you can eke out of moments that used to pass you by.

One of my favorite ways to connect with other people is to write at my favorite coffee house, Café Liquid in Niceville, Florida. I can go there and interact with people if I want, or put on my headphones and retreat into my own little island of creativity: just me and my computer, with Motown playing in my ears while my fingers fly across the keyboard. Conversations are buzzing all around me; connections and positivity resonance surround me like a warm snuggly blanket while I create.

Since I was raised as an only child, I always thought that I preferred to be alone. Unless I was with my family or traveling, my favorite state was hermit-hood. I now realize that I can be with

---

9   *Love 2.0: How Our Supreme Emotion Affects Everything We Feel, Think, Do, and Become:* Page 17, Kindle edition

other people without letting the interaction drain my energy. I don't need to use the "Terri Thing" power until it's all gone. I can replenish it with moments of connection with others. It's amazing how much better my life feels steeped in these moments of shared love; I can't understand how I used to believe that little moments of connection were a waste of time.

I remember when I was deep into the belief that my path to happiness existed in the "make more money and buy more stuff" direction. At one of my lowest points, I responded to a suggestion that I hadn't dealt with a complaint in a caring manner with the phrase, "I've got too much work to do. I don't have time to be nice to people anymore." When these words left my mouth, I knew in my heart they were a lie, but my work-obsessed brain hadn't gotten the message. You can't be a loving parent if you're not connected to love. The good news is that if you practice positivity resonance and connection, you can actually improve your health. My focus on tasks above people led me to migraines and breast cancer, but connection has led me back to balance. I'm living proof that connection not only improves your quality of life, but also the quality of your health.

Dr. Fredrickson's research shows that moments of positivity resonance can improve our health by improving the condition of our vagus nerve, which connects our brain to our heart. One of the functions of the vagus nerve is to quiet our "ancestral fight-or-flight response…it's your vagus nerve that eventually soothes your racing heart, by orchestrating (together with oxytocin) the equally ancestral calm-and-connect response[10]." The measure of how well

---

10 *Love 2.0: How Our Supreme Emotion Affects Everything We Feel, Think, Do, and Become:* Page 54, Kindle edition

your vagus nerve works is called vagal tone; "like muscle tone, the higher your vagal tone, the better.[11] Dr. Fredrickson's research shows that the more you increase your moments of positivity resonance, the more you improve your heart health. Imagine that the small action of connection with others in a positive way can not only enrich your life, but can also prolong it!

Respect *for* others is vastly different than Respect *from* others. When I started respecting myself, by practicing the self-care steps in the previous chapters, it was amazing how much more my kids respected me. My issue with their respect was, in fact, all about me from the beginning. An obsession with gaining respect from others is an indication of being an approval junkie; Martha Beck calls this being "an approval whore."

Because of my drama-addicted parents, my childhood was rarely safe. However, if I could get my parents to like me, then things were calm; nobody was going to threaten death if they were focused on how cute, smart, and funny I was. As long as I played the court jester, and they loved it (and, by association, me), then no one lost their head, either figuratively or literally. That's a very big burden for a little girl: keep your parents' approval or someone will get hurt. I have a feeling that many wolf-babies out there are still operating under the same rules. However, we are all grown up now; we are in charge of our own lives, and we make our own safety. In the words of Dr. Wayne Dyer, "What other people think of me is none of my business. One of the highest places you can get is to be independent of the good opinions of other people."

---

11 *Love 2.0: How Our Supreme Emotion Affects Everything We Feel, Think, Do, and Become:* Page 54, Kindle edition

So how do you rehabilitate an approval ho? By doing for yourself what you think you need from others. If you think you need a partner who understands you before you can be happy, start understanding yourself. The first step toward understanding is self-discovery, and the easiest way to discover yourself is to write down your thoughts. I write my thoughts every morning in my morning pages. Writing down my thoughts of how powerless I feel allows me to take back that power by choosing different actions, instead of waiting for someone else to fix it for me. Without the awareness that comes from seeing these thoughts on paper, you might find yourself at work, sabotaging your job by doing it poorly, because you have a belief that you're not in charge and it doesn't matter anyway.

As children, our days are typically spent in creative play, but as adults, we don't think we have enough time for creativity. I'm here to tell you we do! We all have five to thirty minutes to write three pages of stream-of-conscious thoughts on paper once a day. Just keep your pen moving, even if it's just to write, "This is a stupid waste of time. It makes me so angry that I'm taking time away from important work to do this." What's more important than discovering your own thoughts and then getting them on your side? The most efficient use of your time is to write down limiting beliefs like, "I hate my job, but I have to go to work. What would my mother/boss/Aunt Sadie think if I didn't show up?" Take charge of your life and your thoughts by starting to write them down daily. You have time to spend an hour a day on yourself; you can break it up any way you wish, but include quiet time, sweat time, feasting time, and writing time. You don't have to do the hour all at once; you can break it up into smaller bites of time. As I suggested in the last chapter, if you're starting from scratch, just take five minutes for these important self-care tasks. Remember, putting time aside for yourself is the best way to respect yourself, and this creates a foundation of respect that you can then spread to others.

Another way to show *respect for others* is to stay out of their business. Byron Katie[12] has developed a method of taking control of your thoughts that we will talk about in the next chapter, but her "Whose Business Are You In?[13]" tool is relevant here. In Katie's words, "There are only three kinds of business in the Universe: mine, yours, and God's." You can substitute "Universe" for God if that feels more comfortable. My brief explanation of how I use this tool is: My business is everything that is under my control— my thoughts, my house, my car, what I choose to eat, do, or not do. Your business is everything you choose to think, do, or not do. And God's business is everything else, including: the economy, international unrest, natural disasters, and the existence of reality TV shows (although I believe the last is an unnatural disaster). This includes what's happened in the past, or what may or may not happen in the future. The first step to using this tool is to just notice whose business you're in at any given time. Don't change anything, just notice.

When I started using this tool, I was all up in the business of my kids and anyone else who was close to me. Staying out of the business of others, especially for an approval ho like me, starts with allowing them to have their own business all to themselves. Don't try to make things easier for them before they ask for help.

---

12 www.thework.com/index.php

13 go to www.byronkatie.com/2006/09/whose_business_are_you_minding.htm for Katie's description of this tool.

I was so entwined with my children's needs, that I would help them long before they realized that they had a need. But what I learned, and what I believe is the best way to grow as a person, is to allow them to make mistakes. It's painful for us to see our children fall or fail, but if we never let them fall, they will never have the satisfaction of being able to get back up again on their own. This starts in late elementary school and middle school. When your child has a behavioral problem with another child or a teacher, don't barge in and demand retribution. Talk to your child first about the situation, asking what her responsibility is in the situation. Stick to your family values as a guide, and then go to the teacher or principal if you need more clarification or help. Help your kids learn how to say they're sorry when they make a mistake…more about this in the next chapter.

In my own life the perfect illustration of how this works with older kids is the struggle my middle daughter had with her weight during high school. She was always solid as a toddler and little kid, but never heavy. Then puberty hit, and the curve fairy paid a visit. As she started filling out, my inner chubby kid wanted to protect her from all the heartache I faced, because I had been bigger than all the other girls when I was in middle and high school, and I knew how it felt. So, I pitched a tent in her business: finding "healthy" recipes, frowning at second portions, and encouraging her to exercise "to just be healthy." Since I had weight issues all my life and eating disorders in high school, I made her struggle become Part II of my own. I remember days when I would see her pick up a cookie, and I'd tell her, "Honey, have a piece of fruit instead!" which only made her want to eat eight cookies, just to spite me. Even though I was trying to save her from pain, it wasn't my business. She hadn't even asked me for help; I'd just volunteered because I was the family fixer of all things not perfect. Then I started life coach training and realized what I had been doing. I remember the day I sat her down and told her that her health and weight issues were hers, not mine. I admitted that I was the worst person to advise her on how to lose weight, because I'd spent the last thirty years beating up my body with food. I told her, "I love you with all my heart, but this is your journey, baby, not mine. If you want my help, I'm here…all you have to do is ask."

Then I proceeded to take all the energy I had been pouring onto her and turned it on myself. I began setting a good example for her: going to yoga class, because it made me happy; eating organic foods, because they made me feel better; and eating a couple of bites of ice cream instead of the whole carton. It took a while for both of us to adjust to our new non-symbiotic relationship, and she told me that it was really scary at first to take responsibility for her own struggle. She would try a new diet or exercise and then quit; then she'd try something else and fail. All the while, I was her cheerleader, but she was calling the plays. When she went for her physical before entering college, she had lost thirty-five pounds since her last visit. She is more confident, beautiful (lit-from-within beautiful) and satisfied than I have ever seen her, and she did it all by herself. If I had continued to try and "help" her by staying in her business, I'm not sure she would have ever reached this place…but then again, that's none of my business.

This dance of giving your children support while remaining in your own business changes as your kids age. When they are young, it's completely appropriate to practice the Mommy-Magic of anticipating and filling your children's survival needs. It's up to you to determine their needs before they have language to clearly express them. It's also up to you to decide the difference between needs and desires as they age. When deciding where to step in and where to step back, the best guidelines to use are always your family values and beliefs. If you need to step in to clarify behavior that lines up with your family values, by all means, do so. When your kids get older, usually in middle school, the dance gets a little more complicated. This is where filling your own well and staying in your own business become crucial for your child's development of his own moral compass. This stage is where *showing* him what to do overrides *telling* him what to do. We talk more about this in Chapter Fifteen. If you are filling your own well, you will be less needy. When you fill yourself using the self-care techniques from Chapter 3, then your need to control your kids lessens, and your need to be in their business lessens as well.

Now that you have an idea of how important it is to build up your own self-respect using self-care, the efficacy of seeing artists everywhere, and staying in your own business, let's look at the third R...*Responsibility for your actions.*

CHAPTER FIVE

Responsibility for Your Actions

Responsibility for your actions is something that is woefully lacking in today's fast-paced, "it doesn't really matter who I step on to get ahead" society. You can practice responsibility in many ways. Two of my favorites are: to stand up and apologize when you make a mistake, and to recognize and take responsibility for your negative thoughts. In this chapter, we will look at the power of apologizing, especially to your children, as well as taking the blame to move a situation forward. We will also look at taking responsibility for your limiting beliefs, or as I like to call them, crappy thoughts, which is the first step to changing them.

Being a parent involves making lots of decisions, and decision making is not an exact science. Your kids know that you're human and that you're going to goof up from time to time. The important thing is that you set a good example when you make a mistake. Mistakes are a beautiful learning tool for you and your kids. When you make a mistake, you can thrash and moan, or you can accept the situation, make amends, and move on; which option sounds like a better choice when your impressionable child is watching?

Making an apology sounds simple, but there's more to it than just saying, "I'm sorry." First, there's timing. When you've made a mistake, apologize and make amends quickly. Don't put off facing the music; it will only get louder the longer you wait. A true apology comes with: 1) a verbal recognition of the mistake, 2) a plan to repair it, and 3) a promise not to repeat it. This is especially true if the person to whom you are apologizing is your child. I remember one instance with my bonus child when we were computer shopping. I bought both my high school seniors new computers for their graduation gift. Alyssa was fine with whatever I picked out for her, but Katelyn wanted a more expensive model. She was willing to pay the difference, but I told her it was a waste of money. We got into a long and heated discussion about wasting money, because I could see that she was going into wolf-baby lack mode. This happens when wolf-babies feel like they aren't getting what they need. When you are raised in an environment where you are not valued, acknowledged, or heard, sometimes you assume that other people will never listen to you, so you just give up. This is what happened in this situation.

I acted like a parent, laying down the law when I saw my kid about to make a bad decision, but what Katelyn saw was another adult who wasn't listening to her. It flipped her into lack and attack mode; she felt the lack of support and understanding, so she did her version of attacking: she shut down. This time I wasn't having it; I kept gently prodding her until she spilled the beans. After a lot of time and a few tears, I stopped and just listened to her entire rationale. Her economic rationale still wasn't sound but, after listening, I understood her reasoning. I apologized immediately for not listening completely in the first place and neglecting to give her views their proper weight. I told her I was sorry for making an assumption based upon incomplete information. I also told her that I promised that the next time we were at odds, I would hear her out before making my decision. My decision stood; she still got the less expensive computer, but she felt heard and validated. It was a learning experience for both of us. I realized that she wasn't making a knee-jerk decision based upon her past lack of support (I thought she wanted the more expensive computer just to prevent me from short-changing her...because that's what her experience has led her to expect from adults), and she saw that I loved her enough to admit when I had not supported her emotionally.

Apologies can be powerful tools for connection.

My youngest had an incident in her math class that led to a valuable lesson about taking responsibility. We stayed late at her registration for high school classes, and she forgot that she had a math test the next day. When she realized her mistake, it was too late to study...and she did really poorly on the test. She came home very upset, because math was her hardest class and her lowest grade already, so a bad grade had a big impact. I told her to calm down and just breathe, three deep breaths. Then we crafted a plan. She would take full responsibility for her mistake and e-mail her teacher. This is her actual e-mail:

"Hi Mr. Brown, it's Emily Fedonczak. I REALLY messed up. I take full responsibility for my mistake. I was at Niceville High School's registration last night, and studying for the test completely slipped my mind. I would greatly appreciate it if you let me retake the test. I promise that nothing like this will EVER happen again. I will accept your decision no matter what it is."

Her teacher ended up letting the whole class retake the test, as no one did well on it. I can't be certain that it was Emily's e-mail that resulted in that decision, but it certainly opened up a situation where cooperation could blossom. This is often the result when you take responsibility for your actions.

You want your child to see that it takes strength of character to own your mistakes and learn from them. This is a valuable lesson you can teach to your future great citizen. When you include taking responsibility for your mistakes as part of your parenting plan, not just as a one-time action, then your children will learn that making a mistake is no big deal. This will put them light years ahead of the competition when it comes to the job market. Which leads me to my next *responsibility* tool: take the blame.

In my sales career, especially in the management portion, I have seen the value of taking the blame to move a situation along in various types of conflicts. It doesn't really matter if it's your fault or not, taking the blame in a situation that has reached a stalemate stops the finger pointing and opens the possibility for resolution. The way I take the blame is something like this: "I'm such a dork. I can't believe I did that, but it's done now. What can we do to fix it?" If it really is your fault, this tactic will evoke a sympathetic response in the other person. If you keep stressing how stupid your mistake is, all but a few people will respond with, "Hey, don't worry about it. It's not a big deal." Even if it is sort of a big deal, they will want to minimize it to make you feel better—that's the typical human response.

If you're dealing with a supremely negative person or someone I like to call an Emotional Vampire (someone who sucks the joy out of any situation), this tactic still works. The Emotional Vampire version also involves a little extra time for them to rub in how stupid you are; you just keep smiling and let their negativity run off your back like water off a duck. You don't really care what they think, so let them run out of steam without attaching to anything they say. When you don't react, they will stop…because it's no fun for them if the other person isn't buying into their drama. When everyone is comfortable with the distribution of blame (or, should I say, they are comfortable, because you took it) then you can move onto fixing the mistake.

If, however, you are perpetuating the negative thoughts or beating yourself up for a mistake, then you are embodying your own Emotional Vampire. You must deal with your inner Vampire, or you will never move the situation forward. The holy water for your inner Vampire is Thought Work.

Byron Katie is the originator of "The Work,"[14] a systematic approach to questioning your thoughts. The way I use Thought Work in my practice follows the Martha Beck adaptation of Byron Katie's work. The structure of my Thought Work looks like this:

If you have a thought that causes you pain, question it:

1. Is that thought true?
2. Can you be absolutely sure it's true?
3. Provide three reasons why it may *not* be true.
4. When you think that thought, how do you react?
5. Who would you be without that thought?
6. Find a turnaround thought, and give three reasons why the turnaround thought is as true or truer than the original painful thought.

---

14 www.thework.com

So let's take a nasty thought from the previous section: "My kids don't respect me." I don't really have to deal with this one since I started using self-care to build up my own self-respect, but this thought ate up a lot of my energy in the years before I discovered Thought Work. So let's take this for a walk through The Work.

Thought: My kids don't respect me.

1. Is that thought true?
It sure feels true when they are rolling their eyes and huffing at my every word.

2. Can you be absolutely sure that thought is true?
I can't be absolutely sure, no.

3. Can you give me three reasons why that thought may not be true?
   a) Teenagers roll their eyes at everything, including their best friends, whom I know they do respect.
   b) Rolling their eyes can mean frustration, not lack of respect. Frustration is not about me, it's about them.
   c) My kids still do their chores, are polite, and follow our family values. That shows respect.

4. When you think that thought, how do you react?
When I have this thought, I feel miserly and crabby. I act like Attila the Hun, making rules that are unreasonable, just to show my power. In short, I act in a way that really doesn't deserve much respect. This way of acting makes my own self-respect diminish in the process. By believing this crappy thought, I engage in actions that actually make it more true.

5. Who would you be without that thought?

If I waved a magic wand and was unable to think this thought, I would be calmer. Without worrying about whether or not my kids respected me, I could listen to what's behind the eye roll. I could listen to their frustrations and give them a much-needed sounding board.

6. Find a turnaround thought, and give three reasons why the turnaround thought is as true or truer than the crappy thought.

Turnarounds [15]:

I don't respect me.

    a) I haven't been taking very good care of myself.

    b) I'm not getting enough sleep or exercise, and

    c) I'm not eating right.

I don't respect my kids.

    a) I'm not listening to them, because I'm jumping into battle mode.

    b) I'm not giving them the benefit of the doubt; when people are frustrated, they don't act like themselves.

    c) I'm not a very respectful mom if I'm all caught up in my ego.

My kids do respect me.

    a) They still do their chores, even if they don't like them.

    b) They still say, "I love you, Mom" every time they leave the house.

    c) They still laugh at my jokes; we are still connected.

---

15 Go to thework.com/thework-turnaround.php for more instruction on how to do turnarounds.

If none of the turnaround thoughts make a difference in my mood, then I will come up with a replacement thought that makes me feel better, like, "My kids and I love and respect each other, no matter what." That thought makes me feel light and airy inside.

If I don't use The Work on crappy thoughts, they will hijack my day. When I believe a crappy thought, invariably the feelings and actions that follow that thought will prove it true…just like my lack of respect thought made me act like a dictator who was undeserving of respect. Every time I take a painful thought and run it through The Work, I feel better—every single time. I have run my kids through a brief version of the The Work on problems from test anxiety to mistakes on the volleyball court. It takes time and practice, but every single time you stop a negative thought in its tracks by doing The Work on it, the thought loses its power over you. When it comes up again, you can say, "Hello old friend! I know you're trying to help me in your own bizarre and twisted way, but we are thinking a new thought now." Then substitute your light and airy thought in the space where the old thought used to be. I write the new, airy thought on little notes and stick them in places I will see them often. This has also been very useful for my clients, and I'm pretty sure that the people who sell those little notes are quite happy about it as well!

Taking responsibility for your thoughts and actions, and teaching your children to do the same, is another cornerstone of my parenting plan. I think a parent's ultimate job is to raise good citizens and good employees who become fair employers or successful entrepreneurs. It is our job to prepare our children to become functioning, productive members of society. To do that, you, as a parent, must have the long view. It's not about today; it's about all the days. Taking responsibility for your actions is a basic part of being a good citizen. You want your child to be the first person the boss thinks of when she's looking to promote someone. Warren Buffet was attributed with coining the term "putting skin in the game"[16] as a winning financial strategy, whereby the owners and directors will put money in the company, so that they have a personal stake in whether or not the company is successful. Taking responsibility for your actions when things go wrong is putting skin in the game of your own life.

Every time you make a mistake, and own up to it, you build up your stores of knowledge about what *not* to do; you also build your self-confidence as a risk taker. Change and growth do not happen from a place of safety; if you want to build a better life, and teach your children to do the same, you're going to have to risk failure. Every time you fail, take the energy you would normally put into wailing about how much time you've wasted or how stupid you were and instead turn it toward finding the lesson in why you failed. Take responsibility for the mistake, and then look for the lesson. This way, each failure is a springboard for growth. Every day, I tell my clients, and myself, "Remember, you're exactly where you're supposed to be to learn the lesson you're supposed to learn!" Taking responsibility for your mistakes is the foundation of a discipline practice. And next we look at why rules and discipline are so important in parenting.

---

16 www.investopedia.com/terms/s/skininthegame.asp#axzz28i9YvcT0

CHAPTER SIX

Rules Are Good; Consistent Rules Are Better

Discipline has received a bad rap in the quest to celebrate each child's unique and special qualities. This is all well and good, as long as your child can leave the house without having a meltdown in public. I see kids all the time whose parents don't have a structure in place: no bedtimes, no schedule, and no master plan. These parents are governing their children strictly from Mouse Vision, with no Eagle Vision goals. They don't see the harm in giving in to their three- or four-year-old; they don't think it really matters, because the kid is so small. They don't see the ripple effect that the erosion of discipline has on their children. The kids, as a result, are floundering. They have no respect for adults or rules in general. Why would they? They have no experience living within a structured system. If the parents aren't making the rules *and* sticking to them consistently, then, by default, the kids feel that they are making the rules. That's anarchy. It is our job to equip our kids to be successful in the system that is our society. Whether you live in the Bronx or Bangladesh, a system exists with laws and rules, within which your kids can be successful and happy...if they have the proper tools and training.

When a parent turns over the responsibility of obeying the rules to their small child, they are setting their child up for stress. The child's brain is not developed enough to handle that level of decision making. If you give a five- or six-year-old dominion over their own world without any checks on her behavior, you will turn out a very difficult teenager who is nearly impossible to control. If your tween or teen doesn't play by the rules, he will be very ill-equipped to deal with the job market and relationships as an adult. When your undisciplined young adult tries to pull a temper tantrum on a boss, they won't give your precious lamb a second chance; they will show him the door. Too many applicants are looking for those rewarding jobs to keep an employee who doesn't play well with others.

However, if you raise your young children within a framework of discipline and reward from infancy onward, they will be comfortable maneuvering within a system. There will come a time, in their teenage years, where giving them more responsibility is appropriate, but not before then. Small children, I mean elementary school kids, do not need to be governing their own behavior; it's too much power without enough knowledge to wield it. As your children grow older, you can adjust the rules to pass on responsibility for determining their own course of action, because they now have the tools to make healthy choices.

I hear a lot of parents say that they don't want to discipline their children because they want to be their kids' friend. A parent needs to be their child's ally, and the child needs to know that their parent will be there for them no matter what; but you're not there to be your kid's friend. You're there to be a parent, and sometimes that means you have to be the heavy hand. Occasionally, it's good for kids to suffer a bit of deprivation. Because when they get into the real world and go into the workplace, they will not have everything handed to them because they ask or whine for it. It's a huge shock if they're not trained for this situation at home. It is short-sighted for a parent to set their children up for such disappointment in the real world by giving them everything they want at home.

Little kids, on the whole, crave rules. They crave discipline, because it makes their choices easier. Knowing they don't have to decide if something is a good idea or not is comforting; the rule is "you can't do that." They're too young to realize why that rule exists; all they know is that they are forbidden to break it. And if they do break the rule, the consequences are unpleasant. A pattern of discipline is how we instill family values. Rules and consequences are the delivery method. When your kids are acting according to your family values, they are rewarded. When they stray off the path, they are reprimanded in whatever way you feel is appropriate. Before you know it, they're in college, and your values are their values.

The key to discipline is consistency. As I've said before, many parents make choices not based upon a grand plan that they have for their children, but upon what's easier in the short term. That is a grave mistake. In this section, I will give you tools that have worked for me as part of my parenting plan. In the next chapter, I will give you examples of how discipline changes as your child ages. However, all the tools in the world will not work without consistent application. Discipline and rules make your kids feel safer, and they make you feel more confident. As the parent, you are the leader of your household, or the "general" of your family.

Any general worth her salt will tell you that you must have a plan for any battle if you hope to win and, if you are a parent, you know that disciplining is a series of battles of differing intensity. The upside is that if you have a plan *and* communicate it clearly to your children, then the number of battles decreases exponentially.

It's important to be consistent from day-to-day, but it's also important to have a level of consistency between parents. My therapist/second mom, Dr. Marie Fuller, told me that it doesn't matter if both parents are strict or lenient; as long as the discipline is consistent, the kids will turn out fine. If, however, one parent is strict and one parent is lenient, the kids are ripe for developing anti-social behavior or, in the worst-case scenario, becoming sociopaths[17]. This makes sense if you think about it. If the rules are laid down by one parent and dismissed by the other, the kid learns that rules don't mean anything. Why would you expect that kid to follow any rules in school if there are none at home? That child will follow her whims as they arise, consequences be damned. This is not "good citizen" behavior, nor will it get your child hired for their dream job.

I saw this played out with my was-band. He was raised in an environment where he could do no wrong, with a strict father and a lenient mother. (I'm not a psychologist, and I was not there, so I can't be sure; however, observation of their family dynamic in later years led me to believe this was true.) I don't believe he was ever taught to deal with consequences. As a result, he missed out on over nine years of his daughters' lives, because he was a guest of the

---

17 I am far from an expert on sociopaths, but I do know there is an environmental component to the severity of the disease. If you want to learn more about the sociopathic personality, I highly recommend the book, *The Sociopath Next Door* by Martha Stout, PhD.

Bureau of Prisons. To this day, he maintains that he did nothing wrong. How could he break rules that he didn't believe in? I'm not saying that if you don't have a plan of discipline and apply it consistently that your child will turn out to be a sociopath or go to prison, but why tempt fate? Take responsibility for disciplining your kids; start right now. It's easier when the kids are little, but even if they're bigger, it's worth the battle…I promise. The consequences of not having rules, and enforcing them consistently, are not pretty.

If you don't have a master plan of discipline and reward, at the very least your kids will feel insecure. It doesn't have to be some grand scheme with spreadsheets and flow charts. You just have to figure out what's important to you and then devise a form of discipline that supports that. If you were being interviewed in the future about being a parent, what are the things that you would love to discuss? Imagine your child being a successful and happy adult. What are the rules and beliefs you have now that support that future? What do you have now that should be scrapped in order to make that future a reality? In order to figure out what feels good, you have to actually feel. That means getting out of your brain and into your body. The easiest way to do this is to use a tool we Martha Beck Coaches like to call the Body Compass. This is a tool I use daily on myself and with my clients. The basic application is as follows:

How to Set Your Compass

1. Think of a situation that was very painful for you. Mine is the day that my girls were crying because my wasbund told them that I was solely responsible for our family breaking up. A feeling of extreme frustration arose

because my heart was telling me to leave (and leave now), and my head was telling me that maybe I wasn't doing the right thing…because my kids were so young. Then there were my babies crying right in front of me and looking to me to make it all better…yuck! Put yourself in your painful scene and scan your body for sensation…start at your toes and work your way up to your head. Take your time, and wait for sensation, especially around the area of the stomach and chest. (When I do this exercise, my neck and shoulders tighten, and my chest feels like it's closing. I have trouble breathing. My hands start to sweat, and there's a pounding in my temples.) When you're finished scanning your body, give the strongest sensation a name. That is -10 on your Body Compass. Mine is "Heavy Heart."

2. Shake off the -10 (I'm serious—stand up and shake it off).
3. Now think of a time that was very pleasurable. I always use rocking my kids to sleep. Rocking my babies evokes all the warm, tingly feelings that go along with nurturing. Do the same scan from toes to head. When I put myself in that rocking chair, my chest opens up, and I tingle all over, right up to my scalp. Then name the strongest sensation. I call mine "Tip to Toe Tingles." This is +10 on your Body Compass.

Now you have a built-in divining rod to help you feel your way through a situation that confuses you.

-10 -9 -8 -7 -6 -5 -4 -3 -2 -1 0 +1 +2 +3 +4 +5 +6 +7 +8 +9 +10

On this scale, 0 is a feeling state that is neutral: neither really happy or really sad. As you move toward your +10 feeling, you can actually feel the difference in your body. You will get a warm open feeling. As you move closer to your -10 feeling, you will feel your chest close up and your shoulders move toward your ears. At least that's what happens to me and most of my clients. Now you can use your Body Compass to figure out what's right for you. If you are feeling body sensations that are negative on your Body Compass, notice what you're doing and who you're with. If the same people and situations cause negative sensations consistently, those are the people and situations that you need to avoid in order to maintain a more joyful life. Conversely, spend more time with people who make you feel closer to +10 on your Body Compass.

There's another Martha Beck tool that is closely related to the Body Compass, but it's quicker. If you think about a time when you were suffering from pain that is not directly related to an injury, you feel shackled by your suffering: that's Shackles On. Now think of a time when you felt light and free, creatively inspired or in love with a situation or person: that's Shackles Off. This works for decision making as well. This is a great tool to teach your kids, so that they can easily tune into their body wisdom.

Pick rules for your kids that make your Body Compass feel closer to your +10. My top rules are:

1. Treat others as you want to be treated.
2. Do your homework right after you arrive home from school.
3. Tell the truth, even if it's painful…especially if it's painful. If you have screwed up, you will be punished, but if you lie about it, the punishment will be infinitely worse.
4. Bedtimes and curfews are deadlines, not guidelines.
5. Help those who are less fortunate than you.

6. Don't cheat...others or yourself.
7. You can only watch movies and TV programs that are age-appropriate. (I don't let my kids watch programs or movies that are rated beyond their age-range, because I don't want those images and situations in their head. When they see violence or sex on a screen, they equate that with some semblance of normal, because they aren't old enough to have the discernment capacity of an adult. I want them to stay a kid as long as possible; they have the rest of their lives to be an adult.)
8. Follow your heart, even if it leads you straight into failure. Failure is the best way to learn what not to do. If you never risk, you will never fail...but then what kind of boring-ass life would that be? This may not sound like a typical form of discipline, but learning to risk is the best thing you can teach your child...if you want them to follow their dreams.

The implementation of the rules consistently can be tricky. If your rules say no PG-13 movies before the age of thirteen, because of the questionable content, then your kids don't see those movies, even with their friends. It's a choice that is taken away from them, and you need to explain that to their friends' parents. It doesn't matter if they think you're crazy (and they might), it's the rule. If the issue comes up that the friend's parents have taken your child to a PG-13 movie, because you've forgotten to tell them your rule, don't blame your kid. It's too much pressure for a pre-teen to stand up to a friend's parent. What I did in this situation was to first calm my guilty kid down, and then I called the parent. I apologized for not saying something earlier, but the rule is no PG-13 movies until my kid is actually thirteen. It was a little hairy, but I didn't take it to a place of value judgment about their parenting skills. I just made it about our rule. Then I told Emily to call or text me the next time a situation arises where she knows that following someone else's plan will break one of the house rules. I will be happy to talk to the parent.

If it's a kid who wants her to break the rule, that ball is in her court. This led to a great discussion about how to say "no, thanks" when someone wants you to do something that goes against your values. Saying "no, thanks" with quiet confidence is a skill that will teach your child that rules are something that we own, and they reflect our family values. Discipline is not just something a parent does to a child; it's a way of life. I love the saying that, "Morality is doing the right thing when no one else is watching." If your child picks friends that have the same values and beliefs, the issue of saying "no, thanks" to bad choices won't arise as much. This is why it's so important to be involved in your child's choice of companions. We talk more about this in Chapter Eighteen, but suffice it to say that the more plugged in you are to your kids' lives, the more you will be involved in their choice of friends or, more appropriately, which friends they keep.

I used to have a lot of rules about picking up your room and laying out your clothes at night, because it makes mornings easier, but those are relaxed now that my kids are older. Maintaining those small, nit-picky rules felt bad to my Body Compass, so I dropped them. I highly recommend setting up your own rules, using your Body Compass to guide you. Start with things that are important to you, and then set discipline around those things. I love to travel, and it was important to me for my kids to be polite and well-behaved when we were traveling. So I backed it up and started at home, so they knew that "no" meant "no" within the confines of my own four walls, where the screaming would only bother me. I talk more about this in the next chapter. When my eldest was only two years old, she would ask for something, like this, "Mommy, can I have a piece of candy?"

"Let's eat our veggies first, and we'll see."

She would scrunch up her little forehead and say, "Mommy, how 'bout 'dis deal…I eat my veggies, and you give me two pieces of candy."

"I don't know, Kinsey, two pieces is a lot of candy."

"Mommy, how 'bout 'dis deal? I eat my veggies and you give me four pieces of candy."

Okay, so she was a little weak in math at age two, but you have to give her points for her negotiating skills! I kept thinking she would make a great corporate attorney, but the law does not sing to her. I know that all the time I invested in her discipline turned out a very strong moral compass. She knows when she can push boundaries and when to stop and try a different tack. Even though it's difficult to say, "No" to your kids in the short term, rules set up expectations of behavior; when your kids follow them, your household sails along evenly. When your kids don't follow the rules, it's your job to come up with a punishment that demonstrates consequences for such behavior.

The other thing to remember is when you punish your kids, they will not like it, or you, for a little while…and that's okay. Again, you are not here to be your kid's friend; you're here to be their moral compass until they develop one of their own. When you discipline your children, and they freak out, it has nothing to do with you anymore. Their reaction is their business, not yours (refer back to Chapter Four). You cannot expect to control the discipline *and* the reaction to the discipline. Once you introduce the consequences for an unacceptable behavior, then your only job is to enforce the application of the discipline in a calm, clear manner. This is why it's so important to take care of your own anger first, before you discipline your child. Then you're not taking attention away from the lesson with your own emotions. This is not easy to do when you're in the heat of the moment, hence the need for self-care; when things get emotional, take those three deep breaths and refocus. Sometimes it takes walking out of the room or handing the kid to your partner; do whatever it takes to stay calm and balanced in the midst of the emotional storm of punishment. If you do this, the storm will blow itself out, because you're not adding more emotion to an already charged situation. If you're calm, eventually your child will mirror that calm.

The other thing to remember is to validate your kid's feelings without giving in and scrapping the lesson in the process. If your young child is in time-out for an unacceptable behavior, you can listen to her unhappiness and validate that she is unhappy about the punishment without stopping the punishment. For example:

"Honey, I know you're upset about being in time-out, but this is what happens when you don't tell Mommy the truth. You are in time-out for five minutes, so that you will understand that we don't lie. Remember how yucky this feels the next time you think about not telling Mommy the truth. Even if you've done something wrong, the punishment won't be as bad if you tell me the truth. I still love you, even when I don't love your actions. When your time-out is finished, then you apologize for your actions, and everything will go back to normal."

When you're finished with your explanation, you stop talking or engaging with them. If they break the time-out, you calmly put them right back in it. Keep doing this until the punishment is completed. When it's done, and the child has apologized for her actions, then you're done. Everything resets and returns to normal. This teaches your kids to take responsibility for their mistakes, and that mistakes are not the end of the world.

When you can punish your children without being upset, then let them know that their feelings are valid, even when their actions are unacceptable, then you will be able to steer your kid's moral compass in a way that educates. After that kind of discipline, their behavior can return to normal, and they will still retain the lesson. If you discipline with anger, then your kids will be more focused on your anger than they will their own behavior. They will do whatever it takes to return things to normal without necessarily learning the lesson.

Little kids to pre-teens are more interested in maintaining the status quo than anything else. The more things stay the same, the happier they are, and the more secure they feel. That's why I'm such a proponent of structure; it gives them an expectation of consistency. You can, and should, schedule creative imagination time as well (this works best without a computer screen in front of them). In fact, it's important that the creative, impulsive time happens within a structure, because then they are making choices in places where they are safe and appropriate. For instance, my family loves to craft. When we have the paints and glue gun out, they can go wild...as long as it stays on the paper. The rule is you put down newspaper to protect the table, and then the sky is the creative limit...creative impulse within structure.

Another example is hair. As long as they don't shave their heads, I'm all for some creative license in hair color. My middle child died a pink streak in her hair (of course it was my middle child); I wasn't crazy about it, but I didn't stop her. It was allowed at her school, it didn't hurt her, and she realized after she did it that it wasn't quite as cool as she thought it was going to be. She soon went back and changed it to a blonde streak that went much nicer with her red hair. My eldest thought a tiny nose piercing was the way to go; holes close up, so I said, "Go for it." It didn't last long for the same reason the pink hair went away. Both of these are examples of creative impulse within structure. Our line is drawn at tattoos, because they're permanent. We have told our girls that if they get a tattoo, their sisters will be quite happy splitting their trust fund. If you see my kids in a tattoo parlor, you are welcome to remind them of this fact.

Discipline simplifies the lives of your young children. It leaves them free to live like a kid. All they have to think about is which toy to play with or how much they hate broccoli. That is what kids need to think about; they don't need the stress of making their own rules. They don't need to think about whether it's time to go to bed yet or if they should watch this TV program because it has some questionable language and content. The parent needs to take that choice away from their young child; bedtime is the same time every school night—period. You are only allowed to watch certain channels—period. A plan of discipline evolves with your child as he ages; now we will look at how discipline can grow and evolve as your child does the same.

CHAPTER SEVEN

Discipline through the Ages

In the last few chapters, I've laid out the importance of rules and discipline; I've also mentioned that discipline changes as your kids age. The best parenting plan is one where you set strict behavioral guidelines by consistently enforcing rules with little kids, then change to a fluid framework that allows individual autonomy as your child matures. Just because the framework is fluid, doesn't mean that you give in on the few hard-and-fast rules that remain, however. "No" still means "no"; I just don't say it as often to my teenagers. When your kids are older, the dance of discipline is more complex. Here is how I have successfully applied rules and discipline for my kids in their different stages of development:

Baby to Toddler: Consistency starts here. Baby proof so that your child doesn't think his name is "no." Redirect his attention after saying "no" to unwanted behavior. I remember always taking toys and books to restaurants, because inevitably, someone was grumpy. If they misbehaved, I would discipline them and then re-direct their attention with a game or a toy. If that didn't work, I would take my food to go; there's no sense in trying to force a tired baby to be quiet. It won't work, and you will end up spoiling the dining experience of everybody else. Accept the situation as it is, and leave to try again another day.

The Terrible Twos and Pre-School: If you don't have a discipline routine, mimic what they use in your pre-school. You need to visit the pre-school often, beyond just the pick-up and drop-off, to make sure your child is receiving consistent discipline. If your pre-school doesn't welcome impromptu visits without a legitimate reason (i.e. your visit is upsetting your child's school routine), then find a different pre-school that *is* proud to show off its program to visitors. My favorite form of discipline at this stage is time-out. *Remember: the trick is to apply the discipline without anger.* If you're angry when you discipline your child, she loses the lesson, because she is so focused on her environment returning to pre-anger normalcy. If you discipline your kids in a calm manner, you can still get your point across without losing their focus to fear of your anger.

- Schedules make life easier for your kids; they feel secure when they know what to expect and when. Set up a schedule that works for the whole family and then follow it consistently.

- The mantra at this stage is, "very few rules (based on safety) consistently followed." My eldest went through the terrible twos when she was eighteen months old. We had a rule that you must sit in the grocery cart while Mommy shops, as it was too dangerous to get out of the seat, especially as she had started a "game" of running away as soon as her little feet hit the ground. This particular day had been long, and I was really tired. She started whining about staying in the cart, as we had been in the store for a long time. I told her she must stay in the seat, because *that was the rule*. At this stage that's always the answer to "Why do I have to do that, Mommy?" She was tired, and the whining got louder. If I hadn't had a full cart of groceries, I would have taken her home. Instead, I went to battle stations right there in the produce section, between the bananas and the artichokes. She would whine and stand up, and I would sit her back down, saying, "No, Kinsey, the rule is you must sit in the seat. It's too dangerous to get out of the cart." She stood up, and I put her back down. She kept screaming and, like a WWII Brit, I Kept Calm and Carried On. And then all at once, she gave up. It was a maximum of five minutes, and it was over. She stayed sitting down, snuffling in that post-cry way that will break your heart, and we proceeded to check out. If I had given in to the horrified stares of the other grocery-store patrons, we may have had this scene repeat itself. But since I held fast and stayed calm until I won the battle, now I had a reference point for further skirmishes. When Kinsey wanted to do something that was against the rule, I could say, "Remember that time in the grocery store? When Mommy says, 'no' you're not going to win, sweetie. So give up and let's move on to something more fun."

Elementary School: Schedules are still important, especially since the opportunities for after-school activities increase in elementary school.

- The rule is that homework is completed right when they arrive home while they're still in "school mode."

After homework is completed, all papers and books are reassembled in the book bag, all ready to go for morning.

- Also, bedtimes are the same time every weeknight. When the rules are succinct and clear, and discipline is fair and consistent, your child feels secure. As your kids get older, I would encourage study dates at your house after school. Have yummy nutritious food available and make it a fun atmosphere. This builds the reputation that when kids come to your house, they will be nurtured and fed. For some kids, your house will be the only place that happens. You want to set the expectation in elementary school, so when middle school rolls around, your house is the "it" place. You want your kids at your house, where you know the values and behaviors are acceptable. As always, when other kids come to your house, have your kids explain the rules first, so that a good time is had by all. Let them know in advance that if their friends don't follow the rules, they will be voted off the island.

- Another rule we established in elementary school was to lay out their clothes for school the next morning. You pick two or three outfits and let them choose. That way they have some autonomy within a structure that is approved by you. This also makes mornings go MUCH smoother, especially with girls. Then the morning routine becomes breakfast, dress, grab packed book bag, and out the door.

Middle School: Continue the homework-as-soon-as-you-get-home rule. I also like homework to be done in the family room, especially as computers are now more commonly a daily part of school work. You want your child's computer to be in a public place, just so you can see what he's doing on the internet. I know some net-nanny programs can help protect your child, but there's nothing like the expectation that Mom will be looking over his shoulder to make him think about what he's doing. And that's the best lesson you can teach your kids...to think before they act. It doesn't have to take more than a few moments to think first, but those few moments can save the hours of heartache and pain that come with a bad decision. If someone is asking them to do something that would anger the little Mom or Dad they carry in their head like Jiminy Cricket, then it's a good time for them to say, "No thanks." If they are confused, they can use their Body Compass to see if the decision feels closer to +10 or to -10.

- Since you want your house to be the go-to place for your kids and their friends, it is best if you make the atmosphere fun-filled. When our big girls were in middle school, we added a pool outside and a game room with a big screen for watching movies. This was a big expense, but we were considering it anyway. Do your own version of the game room and the pool, so that your child's friends will always pick your house as the place to hang out.

- Conversely, when your kids go to someone else's house, you need to meet the parents first. This shows your kids and the friend's parents that you care about your child's welfare; it also puts the other parents on notice that you are proactive enough to check up on your kids. Hopefully, this will make those parents a little more attentive to your child while they are responsible for him or her. This is a simple act of love, but you would be surprised at how few people actually do it. I was one of a handful of parents who had this rule in my twenty years of parenting kids.

Remember, middle school is the proving ground for high school. This is the time to begin whittling down your rules to what feels good to your Body Compass, and sticking to the remaining rules consistently. Pick rules that will support your Eagle Vision goals for your child in high school. My rules in middle school were built around systems to make my kids successful academically and establish the kind of friends that they will carry through high school. You want your middle schoolers to establish friendships with kids who support their high school goals and beyond, so there's not an issue of your child's friends pulling her off track.

High School: In high school, the rules reduce even further, with the focus still on family values.

- I kept a few rules that were strictly enforced, such as "no" means "no." Lots of room for debate exists with a "maybe," while "no" remains firm. The things that I say "no" to in high school are really safety issues. Like this: "You don't go to a party if the parents aren't home, because that's when life-altering stuff happens. You always text me the name of the parents whose house you're visiting as well as the address, so that I know where to come find you if things go wrong." I also require my kids to text me the address when they change locations; I love texting, because my kids can communicate with me without their buddies thinking that they're lame. I want to know where my kids are at all times. It's not that I don't trust my kids; it's just that I don't trust other kids. They weren't raised by me, and they may have vastly different value systems. I don't want their values, or lack thereof, to put my child in danger.

- Another high school rule is "a curfew is a deadline, not a guideline." Our rules about curfew are well-known. We had a friend of my bonus kid stay with us during her senior year in high school. The friend's mom and I worked out a curfew structure that we were both comfortable with, and I communicated it to our guest. I guess she didn't believe me or my daughters when we told her that the curfew was a deadline. The first night she went out, she got home fifteen minutes late, and she was grounded for the rest of the week. I didn't apologize, because that was the rule. She ended up calling her mom and choosing to stay at someone else's house with different rules, and that was fine. The funny thing to me was my bonus kid's response; she was mad at her friend for breaking the rules. Then she warned her not to bad mouth me because of said rules. She made her friend feel really bad about the whole thing. I just gave her friend a big hug and reassured her that everything was just fine. I wasn't mad at her, but I was also not changing my rules. If you establish a loving environment filled with fun, your kids will not want to upset that peace by breaking your rules, especially if the rules are fair, explained clearly, and consistently enforced.

- We also continue the "homework right when you get home" rule all the way through high school. I didn't follow my kids around to make sure they were doing their homework, but they were expected to finish homework before social media sucked them in. I encourage my kids, and the high schoolers that I speak with, to turn off their phones and close out all social media when they are studying. They can use social media as a break when they lose focus in their studying. When they are using their social media treats, they set an alarm to make sure it doesn't eat into their study time. When the alarm goes off, they go back to studying until they get tired again, and then they take another break. This way, you're not telling them to stop all social media; you're giving them the reins to arrange a schedule that works for them. It's creativity within structure except that they are creating their own structure, and that autonomy might just mean they will follow their plan. If it doesn't, it's not your business anyway!

You may not think that small skirmishes are important, but they are. If you win the small battles when your kids are little, then the real battles (smoking, drugs, drinking, and sex) will be so much easier. You know the old phrase, "Little kids, little problems; big kids, big problems." Doesn't it then make sense to establish a system of discipline that makes it very clear to your kid who is in charge while their problems are still small? Isn't it better to lay down the law, with your kids respecting you as sheriff, while they are too small to know that there is any other way?

When my fourteen-year-old was six, she and I had a running conversation in which she constantly tried to outmaneuver me. She whined and cried that I was being unfair, and I knew that if I just did it her way, it would make things much easier (and I do mean *much* easier; this kid has an iron will!). When she pushed me, I would say, "Emily, when you and Mommy fight, who always wins?"

To which she mumbled, "You do."

I would then respond, "Right, so why bother fighting anymore? Aren't you tired of fighting? Wouldn't it be a whole lot more fun to do it my way, and then let's go play a game? You know Mommy's not going to say 'yes' once she's said 'no,' so give it up!"

Sometimes she would protest a little while longer, but if I said the same thing over and over in a calm tone, she eventually gave up. The efficacy of this tool was proven just the other day with her sister.

I was having a verbal fencing match with my middle child, when my bonus girl said, "Give it up, Alyssa. You know that you're not gonna win once Mom has said 'no,' so why don't you just save your breath." I was all dug in for WWIII, but when she said this, the battle evaporated. What a treat! It's been so satisfying to find that my system of parenting doesn't only work with my biological children; it has allowed a blossoming of self-confidence and humor in a kid that was guarded and prickly (for good reason) when she came to us. She went from being a boarder who we only saw for meals to a full-fledged wacky member of our family circus.

Consider the weight of this responsibility the next time you are tempted to give in on a battle with your kids that you know you should stick with until you win. Sometimes it's so tiring being a parent; it's easier just to let them stay up past bedtime or go to the mall with that friend who you think is a little morally shaky. Your kids are looking to you to set the parameters of their behavior.

They don't really want to be in charge (no matter how many times they roll their eyes at your rules). They just want the space to play and develop their own unique personality—a personality that develops from an inner desire, not a social need to be just like everyone else.

CHAPTER EIGHT

Want Vs. Desire and Delayed Gratification

The Social-Self/Essential-Self struggle is a concept that Martha Beck introduced in the first chapter of her groundbreaking book *Finding Your Own North Star*. Martha defines your Social Self as, "the part of you that developed in response to pressures from the people around you, including everyone from your family to your first love to the pope." She defines your Essential Self as, "the personality you got from your genes: your characteristic desires, preferences, emotional reactions, and involuntary physiological responses, bound together by an overall sense of identity. It would be the same whether you'd been raised in France, China, or Brazil, by beggars or millionaires." The difference between want and desire is very similar to the difference between your Social Self and your Essential Self, or as I like to call them, your Inner Judge and your Inner Guide. Since your Inner Judge is forever comparing you to other people, she can make decisions from a state of lack or want. If you live your life in a state of want (I want this. I want that. I wanna be thinner, prettier, or richer), then you will communicate that to your children; in turn, they will spend their lives in a state of want. "Want" in our society is usually fulfilled by material or superficial things. Desire is a different animal. It comes from a place of inner space. Desire comes from a seed that's planted in your heart. When we follow our Inner Guide desires, they can lead us to venture into wondrous new places. Because desire comes from within, it comes from our bodies. Want is totally a mind thing. If you live in a state of want, you will continually make fear-based decisions, as want is based in a fear of lack.

I believe that fear-based lack is from the caveman days when avoiding famine was necessary for survival. Since we didn't know when, or if, the next feast would appear, we lived in fear of famine. In today's world, famine is not the norm. Not in North America anyway; we're pretty flush. I know thousands of people go hungry in cities across the nation, but that's not what I'm talking about; this is about those who have enough money to put three squares on the table and a roof over their head, yet it's not enough. They want the next new toy, or the newest gadget to keep up with the neighbors, and they will put their family into crushing debt to get it.

When the Inner Guide and the Inner Judge are in balance, the former determines the direction you're going and the latter provides the guardrails. Your Inner Guide uses "desire" to pull you in a direction that "feels" right. The Inner Judge wants to mold your life to look similar to everyone else's, in order for you to fit in with the group. Fitting in is not always bad. Since we live within a society with systems and rules, listening to your Inner Judge may keep you from appearing in front of a different kind of judge. When your Inner Judge is benevolent, she helps you move within systems most effectively. We run into trouble when our Judge becomes more of a "hanging judge," because in that instance the first person she looks to hang is your Inner Guide. Your Inner

Guide only speaks the truth, and truth can be dangerous if it goes against the societal norms that your Inner Judge holds so dear. In caveman days, if you didn't fit in, you would be shunned from the circle around the fire. Your Inner Judge believes that the group will keep you safe from the saber-tooth tiger...bless her little Neanderthal heart! However, does this model make sense in a world where our biggest threat is often a computer virus? It's not only a problem because the concept is archaic and outdated, it's also dangerous when the Judge muzzles the Guide's desires with the imperative to buy or do things to fit into a mold that makes the Inner Guide wither. You cannot live your right life without your Guide's desires pointing you in that direction. It will be a shiny facsimile of your right life, but it will never feel truly authentic. This is where I found myself in my commercial real estate job. I was making great money with a big office and a view, but my Inner Guide was withering and taking my health with her.

Some will tell you that living in a state of want is motivating (these people are mostly sales types who've built a life around selling people stuff they don't need. I used to be one of these people, so I'm speaking from experience). But is this really true? Have you ever made a loving, balanced decision from a state of lack? This only works when the goal is the next shiny object you *think* you need to fit in and be happy. Happiness, true happiness, doesn't reside in things; it resides in connection with other people. Happiness as a goal comes from the seed of a desire to connect. The goals that come from that seed are to be a kinder person, to spend more time with our children and other people we love, who love us in return. These goals can be fulfilled with just a narrowing of our attention and energy. All you need is a focus that turns away from electronic gadgets and social media toward person-to-person relationships. This is the stage where desire plays a starring role.

In order to teach your kids the difference between want and desire, you have to believe it yourself. When was the last time a new pair of shoes gave you a hug or made you feel better about yourself for longer than the time it took to put them back in the box? I know you think something shiny and new will make you feel better, and maybe it does for a little while...maybe you are flush with the newness and the attention from other shoe junkies (have you seen the pictures on my website? I've been in the belly of the beast, people). But how long does that flush last? When it wears off, before you start searching for the next purchase to get the rush back, isn't there a moment of sadness and despair? A moment when your Inner Guide whispers, "How many shoes will it take to make you happy? If you don't know, I do. There aren't enough shoes in all of Nordstrom to make you happy, because you're looking for love, not stuff."

When you listen to that inner voice and follow your desire instead of your want, it will lead you to some form of connection: a dance class, a knitting group, a coffee shop filled with people who laugh at each other's jokes. You have to experience it for yourself before you can teach it to your children. How do you narrow your focus to find your desire? First you must be still and quiet in order to hear the little voice of your Inner Guide. It doesn't take a long time, but you do need to stop all the chatter in your head at least once a day. Many meditation tapes out there can float you off to a world of stillness. My two favorites are "Yoga Nidra" by James Jewell and "The Soul of Healing Meditations" by Deepak Chopra.

The Yoga Nidra meditation is done in corpse pose, so all you have to do is lie there and let the music and his lovely voice guide you (I think he sounds just like Professor Snape in the Harry Potter movies, so I had to get past that image before I could really focus) into a deep relaxation. The Deepak Chopra meditation is broken into shorter pieces, so that's a favorite if I only have ten to fifteen minutes to meditate.

My stillness practice is not always without movement. Sometimes, I go outside and watch the water flow past me in the bayou behind my house, or I listen to other meditative music while I walk. The only thing that remains constant in my meditation practice is a gentle steering of my hamster-on-a-wheel brain toward a place of no words. Each time I have a thought, I say to myself, "thinking" and then gently let it float away. In this state of deep relaxation, I have come up with my best ideas and brainstormed solutions to problems that seemed insurmountable. I will come up with desires that I didn't know I had, all because I stopped the words that are ever-present in my writer/speaker's brain. Since I make my living with words, taking a break from them seems counterintuitive. However, every time I stop and let my mind be still, I can come up with better and clearer ways to express my desires, thereby making them easier to form.

Another coaching tool that I use to narrow in on my desires is the Body Dowsing tool. Martha Beck introduced this tool in her book *Finding Your Way in a Wild New World*. It's another body-centered tool like the Body Compass, but it's much simpler. The gist is that you are building another compass to steer you in the direction of your heart's desire, using your Inner Guide's wisdom instead of your Inner Judge. The way I use this tool is as follows:

a) Stand up straight and tall, centered on your feet with your hands at your sides, and close your eyes.

b) Take three deep breaths and then say the word "pain" either aloud or in your head. Notice which way your body leans. This is your negative response. If there's no movement, take three deep breaths, from your stomach, and try again. Keep breathing and trying until your body tilts in some direction.

c) Then stand straight again, take a couple of deep breaths and say the word, "peace," either out loud or in your head. Notice which way your body leans. This is your positive response.

When you have a dilemma (or even a relatively insignificant choice) that is demanding a decision, try dowsing the answer. Hold both choices in your head and say one of the choices aloud, then notice which way your body tilts. If it's in your positive direction, go with that choice; if it's negative, then dowse the other choice. If you get a negative on both choices, perhaps the right choice for right now is to rest. Always make rest one of your choices; it's the best choice when you're feeling overwhelmed. Maybe you just sit and breathe for five minutes and start all over again. You can use this throughout your day to streamline your thoughts.

I used to spend minutes (or hours) agonizing over the right choice in everything from which clothes to wear to an important event to what I wanted to eat for lunch. Since I was so out of touch with my body at the time, my mind would wrap me up with doubt and "What ifs." Now I body dowse everything. My positive is a forward tilt and negative is backward, but I've had clients tilt left for negative and right for positive. It's your tool, customized for your body. Start with small decisions at first, then progress to decisions with greater import. The crucial thing to remember is to accept the decision and move on; don't keep dowsing and dowsing "just to be sure." That negates the power of the tool. This one tool will conserve tons of energy that you used to spend on doubting your decisions; then you can use that energy to move forward on the path to your right life.

If you wait for your kids to come to you with a dilemma, and then teach them how to use their body to make decisions, one of three things will happen: 1) They will have one more example of how crazy their parents are, and they will dismiss the tool and, by association, you, 2) They will think you're crazy and then file the tool away to use in private, or 3) They will try the tool and think it's cool and, by association, that you're cool, too. Whichever of these scenarios happens, it's okay, because it's none of your business. Your business stopped at the introduction of the tool; what they choose to think or do with it is up to them. By the way, if you would like to blame the craziness of closing your eyes while you notice which way your body tilts on me, feel free. My whole family already thinks I'm crazy.

The more you can teach your kids that happiness is not something that can be bought, it's something that develops naturally from a life filled with experiences that rate close to +10 on their Body Compass, the less they will be drawn to the "I can only be happy if I have as many toys as my friends" thinking. I used to buy into that thinking, no pun intended, but, since I became a life coach, things have changed. That doesn't mean that I don't buy my kids stuff anymore; it's just not the priority it used to be. I see now that it's more valuable to instill a sense of resolve and determination than to buy them what they want, when they want it. Your kids will need resolve and determination to find their own path in this very confusing world of apathy and chronic short-term thinking. Sidebar while I climb on my soapbox:

When was the last time you called someone to repair something in your home and had them arrive on time or even call you back? There is a critical lack of competent, caring artisans in the workplace today, and I think it relates back to a lack of competent parenting. If my kids didn't call someone back or show up when they promised, I would have their heads. In our home, you don't make promises you can't keep. If you say you will do something, then you do it. If something unforeseen happens to impede the fulfillment of your promise, you take responsibility for the screw up, even if it's not your fault (refer to Chapter Five for a refresher on taking responsibility).

I remember when my middle child forgot to drop a class in her collegiate high school. She listened to her friends instead of checking for herself, thinking that her absence from class would automatically drop her...not so much. She came crying to me late one evening, because she had checked her grades, and she had an F in that class...AN F! We are a straight A, maybe an occasional B, household; an F was worthy of midnight tears. I told her to go talk to her guidance counselor without blaming it on anyone else; take responsibility for her screw up and find out the best way to fix it. She tried to get me to do it for her, but I told her it wouldn't mean as much if I fixed it; she was sixteen years old...she could do this. So she went to the counselor, and she had to take the class over again; the same class she could've dropped without penalty, if she had taken the time to investigate things for herself. It was a hard-earned lesson, but you can be sure she became responsible for her own grades thereafter. She also discovered that she really did care about being a good student. She tried to affect apathy in order to be some weird semblance of cool, but deep down she cared. That was the best lesson of all. Okay, stepping down from the soapbox, now...

The only way to instill resolve and determination into your children is to make them tough. The only way to make them tough is to let them suffer a bit. I'm not talking about putting them through some sort of baby boot camp; I am suggesting a bit of deprivation: delayed gratification, to be exact. This is a big buzz phrase in our house. It's also extremely difficult to enforce, especially in today's "I want it now" society. My kids moan because their friends get everything months or years before they do. If my kids want something just because Janie next door has it, that's not a good enough reason. If they demonstrate that they have a real desire that will be met if I buy them something, and there's a birthday or Christmas coming up, then I will put it on the list of options. I tell them that they will appreciate the gift all the more, because they waited for it. In response, they shake their heads and mutter under their breath as they leave the room. Just like disciplining, I don't give in. Delayed gratification is part of our family values, and the demonstration requires consistent application. The more consistent my application, the quicker the moans will stop. My youngest has found a way around this rule;

she will ask me what chores she can do for money, and then she pays for it herself. That's fine! I have a rule that no matter how much money my kids earn, if they put it in their savings account, I will match it. If it's in their wallet, it's up to them what they spend it on; no matching grant for wallet money.

You can teach delayed gratification in all sorts of ways. With small children who have no sense of time, the answer to "Mommy, can I have xyz?" is "Not now, honey. I'll give it to you next Tuesday." They have no idea when next Tuesday is; it just gives them an answer they can live with. As they grow, your answers become more sophisticated, or simpler, as the case may be. The thing to remember when your child asks you for something for the eleventy-ninth time is that "no" is a complete sentence. I don't mean to say that it's a popular sentence or one that's easy to enforce, but it is a perfectly acceptable answer. As I've said before, in my house I reserve "no" for the final judgment, since it is the final answer.

I usually say "maybe" or "we'll see," which is code for my kids to develop and deliver a concise and thoughtful argument; the better the argument, the closer they are to receiving a "yes." This teaches them important life skills: determining what they want and crafting a plan to get it. Some of my best parenting moments have been sitting and listening to my intelligent and hilarious children crafting arguments that always amuse me and quite often win me over to their way of thinking. But not after I've said "no." They know that "no" is the signal to give up and move on. That's why I'm very careful to think about why I'm saying "no." I keep "no" for things that don't line up with our family values. For example:

Teenager: "Mom, can I go spend the night at Katie's house? She's having a party."

Me: "Are her parent's home?"

Teenager: "I don't know."

Me: "If her parents are home, yes, you can go to the party and spend the night, but I need a verbal from the parents that they will be home. If no parents, then no party and no sleepover."

I don't care if this makes me unpopular, I'm not here to be my kids' friend; I'm here to be their parent.

It's easier to say "no" to your kids if you're very clear on the difference between want and desire. Teach them that they will get a "yes" more often if they can demonstrate a desire-based question. For instance, my bonus daughter loves to paint. I didn't know this until my middle child mentioned it. Since my new girl is a bit reticent about asking for things, I approached her about suggestions for birthday presents. She said that she didn't really need anything, to which I replied, "What do you really want, all the way down to your toes? Alyssa tells me that you like to paint." Her eyes lit up, and she said that art supplies would be fine. The words were nonchalant, but the light in her eyes was the first bit of sparkle I had seen since she came to live with us. She also said that she would like some clothes and accessories, but there was no sparkle when she said it. So she got a boatload of art supplies and one or two pieces of clothing. I am still teaching her to follow her sparkle, in spite of her tendency toward lack-based thinking.

This "putting your money where their heart is" teaches your kids to discover their true desires. Kids are much better than adults at listening to their Inner Guide; they've had less time to acquire a forceful Inner Judge to drown out the Guide's whispers. Your Inner Guide doesn't shout its desires; you have to be quiet and listen. When your Guide speaks, it whispers in short directives, and it's never critical; it says "Rest. Play. Go talk to that person; they will help you find your way." If you're confused about which voice is talking to you, notice the phrasing and tone. If the voice in your head is telling you how stupid you are or talking in paragraphs about what you need to do RIGHT NOW in order to stay safe, then it is your Judge. That doesn't mean that you ignore everything it says, only the part that makes you feel icky and small.

Teach your kids the difference between the two selves, and they will be better able to manage their self-talk. Directing their own self-talk leads them to a sense of balance and self-efficacy. If you can teach them to follow their inner directions to discover a deeply held desire, they will be much happier and less likely to let other kids talk them into doing something that goes against that heartfelt desire. The more often you can build your family values around deeply held desires, the more you can give your kids the tools to point their lives in a direction that makes them truly happy.

Teach your children to make good choices for themselves by using discipline based upon family values and delayed gratification, in order to make them appreciate the things they have. Then the odds that they will be led into a bad choice, by someone who has different values, drops dramatically. It makes my heart hurt when I see a child with no backbone being led into bad behaviors, just because she is wandering with no direction; she will go in whatever direction the most seductive person pulls her. And those seductive users often come from homes where the only attention they receive is from correction for negative behavior. I talk more about protecting your kids from these soul suckers in Chapter Eighteen. Their goal in life is to pull other kids into their pain. You're not going to stop it; the only brake will be your child saying, "No, thanks." As your kids get older and can choose for themselves what to do and what not to do, your values and their respect for them will ensure that they will pick the kinds of friends who support their inner desires. These will be friends with positive goals who are on a path to making a difference, not friends who just want to sit around, smoke dope, and listen to bad rap (is there such a thing as *good* rap?).

If you can create a home environment that is positive and filled with things that support Inner Guide desires, then you will have a welcoming place where all the kids will want to visit. You will also create a place where your kids will want to stay because no place else makes them feel quite as loved and understood. When you create a home that feels like a hug every time you walk into it, then your child will be much more conscious of keeping that sense of peace by following your rules and upholding the family values. How do you do that on a limited budget? I thought you'd never ask!

CHAPTER NINE

Family Values
Create a Happy Home

In a few words, traditions establish an expectation of stability, and stability is something that wolf-babies don't come by naturally. That's why we practice it by establishing traditions. Kids, even older kids, love traditions and stability; even if they roll their eyes at you, inside, they're delighted with the idea that something in their life remains constant. If you give them a happy home life, complete with traditions, they will do everything in their power to keep the status quo. Be cognizant of this fact before you fly off the handle trying to improve family traditions that may be better left alone. I saw this played out Halloween before last when I put off decorating. We were still mourning the death of my mother-in-law, plus I didn't have time to decorate before leaving town for a few days on life-coaching business. When I returned, there was only a week left until Halloween, so I thought, "Why bother? Nobody will really care." You'd think I would know better, but this is why I'm a parenting coach; when I screw up, I can help you through the same thing! Because our house wasn't decorated for fun, my little one decided to go trick-or-treating at her friend's house. I didn't decorate or dress up, and it sucked. When I talked with all of my girls about it after the fact, we all agreed that decorating for Halloween is part of our family tradition, and we will uphold tradition, timing be damned. My new college freshmen carried on our family tradition by carving pumpkins at college and dressing up without me.

Family traditions give kids something to look forward to, and they build a consistent expectation of fun year-round. Decorating for the holidays peaks at Christmas. I have many big boxes of Christmas decorations that we empty each year the day after Thanksgiving, thereby transforming our house into a winter wonderland. This year, my housekeeper bore witness to this tradition and told me later how amazing it was to see us all decorating together like a swarm of Christmas carol-singing bees. She said that she didn't see people pulling together as a family like that anymore. It makes me smile just to think of all of us hanging ornaments and distributing Santas and garland about the house. We have so many decorations that the whole shebang takes the six of us about two hours; and it usually includes a scuffle over who is stuck with fluffing the garland and the ginormous fake tree (we can't have real trees because of allergies). When we are finished with the decorating, sometimes we pull out the Christmas crafts, and sometimes we collapse in a heap in front of the big screen to watch *Elf* or *It's a Wonderful Life* (I always vote for the latter as the best Christmas movie ever, but *Elf* usually wins that contest).

Christmas decorating and crafting are only some of our traditions, another is the family vacation to someplace exotic in the summer. We have been to Europe, Belize, the Dominican Republic, and the Bahamas, and this past summer we went to Africa. I love watching my kids absorb other cultures and steep themselves in other cultures. It not only gives them an appreciation for what we have, but also a realization that there are other ways to live and love; this expands their minds to the vastness of life's experiences But you don't have to take your family to some place overseas; even a visit to an organic farmer's market, a temple, or a monastery can demonstrate other cultures and values to your kids. Heck, you can just go to a restaurant that serves authentically prepared food from another country to broaden their experience.

Another tradition that keeps me connected with my kids is to make them lunches or snacks where I include a little love note. Even if they don't want me to make them lunch, they still get a note. The notes vary in content depending upon relevant topics and my level of mirth, but they're always signed, "I Love You, xoxo, Mom." The notes have become so popular, that I'm now writing notes for my ninth grader's lunchroom mates. For a while, I was writing notes for two high school seniors, one middle schooler, and three of her friends; this put my funny meter to the test! When I'm traveling, my husband continues the tradition, except he can draw. Last month, he proudly exclaimed that my youngest daughter's best friend wore his note on her shirt all day, because she thought it was so cute. If this appeals to you, try it. If it doesn't, come up with another way of showing your children that you love them, and you're thinking of them when they aren't with you. Your kids will respect you more, and they will think of your love before making a decision that might taint that love in any way. It doesn't matter what traditions you follow; the point is that you follow them. Traditions give your kids the opportunity to identify with your family values…to feel special. In addition to building family traditions, you can follow a few simple guidelines that help make home life easier and your family happier. After all, a happy home life leads to happier, well-adjusted kids.

If I had to sum up our family mission statement, it would be: *Just do the right thing*. I tell my kids that sometimes it seems hard to do the right thing, but, in the end, it's infinitely simpler. The day-to-day practice looks like this: if you just tell the truth, be kind, respect your fellow man as well as yourself, and take responsibility for your screw ups, the right thing is the only real choice. You don't have to keep track of what white lies you told to whom. The truth will literally set you free from worrying about when that evasion or lie will come back to haunt you. Decisions about what to do when faced with a temptation like drinking or drugs become easier, because your kids know that's not the right thing to do.

I will never forget when my oldest was about two-and-a-half, and we were at the grocery store with her baby sister. I was sleep deprived and missed paying for a box of crackers…it was under the diaper bag. I had already buckled everybody in the car and unloaded the groceries when I found the box. I really didn't want to go back and pay for that stinking box of crackers, but it was the right thing to do. So I got everybody back out of their car seats, and hauled them and the box of crackers back inside the store to pay for it. The customer service person was stunned that I had come all the way back to pay for one box of crackers, but I said to her, and Kinsey overheard, "If I left without paying, that would be stealing…and we don't steal. We do the right thing." The woman took my money and shook her head, but I could see the click in Kinsey's brain as the lesson sunk in. It wasn't the easiest choice, but it was the right one.

Coming up with your own set of family values is the first step to building a parenting plan and creating a happy home. I've said before that kids of all ages crave consistency; a happy home is one where they know what to expect. Family values are the structure around which you can build consistent expectations. When your child questions why we are doing it the hard way, you can say "Because we're the good guys, and that's how we do it. Sure it's easier to not stand up for your beliefs and just follow the crowd, but in the long run you are cheating yourself. We do it the kind way, because we don't cheat other people…and we especially don't cheat ourselves." In this way, you build a shield of values that your child can use when he or she is dropped into a pit of emotional vampires in middle or high school. She can just say "no thanks," because she has your value shield to protect her.

Time together is at the core of my parenting plan, and I have various ways to make that happen. I've already talked about the importance of family dinners together, but you can spend time with your kids in other ways that instill family values and inject some fun into the house. In addition to Christmas crafts every year, we do a family game night that is consistently hysterical. A few years ago, my youngest came up with "Outback Thursday." Every Thursday, we would eat on the porch out back (get it?) and then come inside to play Scattergories or Life. It doesn't matter what traditions you create, just pick some that sound like fun and reflect your family values. We have a tradition of crafting, because I know that making something with your hands is grounding. I don't care how bad my day has been, when I sit down to knit or bead a necklace, I feel better. Creativity is one of the most powerful ways you have of connecting with your Inner Guide, and it's also a powerful way to connect with your kids. If there's an expectation of creativity as a family, it becomes an anchor for your child that they can take with them when they leave your house. I think that's why my two college freshmen carved pumpkins—it was fun, and it reminded them of home.

Traditions are about a sense of security; your kids know that Christmas is coming because the glue and glitter come out of the closet. They know the holidays are coming because the Halloween decorations go up (at least they will without fail from now on!). When my bonus child came to live with us, I asked her if she had any traditions in her family. She shared a Christmas Eve tradition that her mom had, and we incorporated it into our Christmas. You can borrow ideas for starting traditions from Pinterest or Google, just start some today…your kids will thank you for it.

The next tool to creating a happy home is to have a sense of humor…the wackier the better. There's nothing so serious that you can't poke fun at it. When I was diagnosed with breast cancer, and I knew that I was having a mastectomy in a couple of weeks, I did what any cancer patient would do: I had a bon voyage party for my breast. We sent out invitations to everyone we knew to join us at our "Tah-tah to the Tata" celebration. I know this is a little crazy and bordering on blasphemous, but I thought cancer was pretty insane and blasphemous as well. This wacky approach gave my family a humor handle on a situation that left us all feeling powerless. We might not be able to cure cancer, but we can sure as hell laugh at it. That doesn't mean I didn't cry as well, because I did; however, my coping mechanism of laughing at cancer gave me a little toehold to use on the climb back to feeling like a whole person again. As a parent, don't forget to also laugh at yourself…

loudly and often. It teaches your kids that humor is a very freeing way of handling tough times; in fact it's the best coping mechanism for fear in all its many forms.

We value humor in our house more than just about anything, and we each put a lot of energy into being the funniest person at the dining room table. As a result, our house is filled with laughter. You, as the parent, set the standard for humor in your home. Being a parent is the most important job you will ever have, but it doesn't have to be serious. You can teach lessons with humor much easier than you can with force. Discipline can also be done with humor. When you have self-respect (that you've built up from a practice of self-care), then you know that your rules will be followed. You don't have to be mean to get your kids to do what you say; they do what you say because that's the rule. If they don't follow the rules, then the consequences they experience will not be so much fun…. but you still don't have to be mean about it.

This reminds me of a time last summer when we were on a family trip in Europe. We had a long layover in the Barcelona airport, and I was hungry. I had ventured to one of the airport restaurants in search of gluten-free sustenance while my family had pizza, when I saw that they had Pringles for sale. My youngest is a Sour Cream and Onion Pringles fanatic, and I thought they would be a treat for her, as she hadn't had any Pringles for the two weeks we had been in Europe. The restaurant had Plain and Tomato (ewww!), so I bought the Plain. I almost skipped back to our seating area, smiling ear-to-ear. I whipped out the can with a flourish and said,

"Emily, look what I got for you…Pringles!"

To which she made a face and retorted, "Yuk! Didn't they have Sour Cream and Onion? I don't like the plain kind."

Instead of smacking her for her ingratitude, which crossed my mind, I said, "Wrong answer. Since you are so ungrateful as to turn your nose up at my generous offering, you get no Pringles today, sassy pants."

When you are given a gift in our family, you show appreciation, even if the gift isn't exactly what you wanted; the thought of the giver is worthy of a smile and a thank you. So, I made a big show of passing around the can to everyone else in the family while making long and loud yummy noises. Before long, Emily was saying how sorry she was, and she would never turn up her nose at my gifts again; she went further to draw me a picture of a Pringles can with "I Love You, Mommy" surrounded by hearts. For this, she earned one chip. Could I have gotten mad at her to "teach her a lesson" in how you're supposed to treat your parents? Yes, I could have. But I chose humor to do the job instead, and we still refer back to that scenario when she starts to get a little lippy. It's amazing how quickly she pops back to her loving, grateful self!

Beyond establishing traditions, using humor, and preaching gratitude, the best way I know to assure a happy home is to tell my kids all the time how lucky I am to be their mom. I say, "I thank God every day for giving you to me. I'm so glad you're my daughter." Even when I'm mad at them, especially when I'm mad at them, I tell them I love them. I love them enough to set patterns of behavior that I know will help them in their future lives, and I love them enough to say "no" when "yes" would put them in a situation I know is bad for them. When you think about how much you love your children, say it aloud; this goes double for your spouse. Also, don't let your kids pass you by without hugging them. This will teach them that affection is a normal part of life, and a relationship just doesn't feel right without it. This will eventually shrink the pool of life partners to those who are kind and affectionate. Hopefully, this will reduce the chances that your daughter or son ends up with an emotional vampire as a partner. I know I mention emotional vampires a lot (I've devoted all of Chapter Eighteen to a field manual), but it's only because I've spent so much of my precious time, money, and love on them in the past. I have always tried to pour as much love on my kids as I could, in the hope that they will see that situation as normal. Then when someone doesn't treat them with the same respect and love, hopefully, my girls will just leave, instead of interpreting that lack of love as a response to an internal deficiency...like I did.

Creating a happy home life is of prime importance in my parenting plan. When your house is happy, your kids can find respite inside that happiness, no matter what their school or social life is throwing at them. This doesn't mean that we don't have disagreements in our house, because we do have four opinionated females and one male who must sometimes shout to be heard. Fortunately, he doesn't have a need to be in charge, and we don't have a need to be told what to do. We all do a kind of "I need this," "I can give you that," and "please help me" dance with each other; we respect each other while defending our positions when we disagree.

This was not always the case, as I used to be much more concerned with making my kids toe the line as proof of how powerful I was. That was a big mistake. As I've related in Chapter Three, this was the result of taking very poor care of myself and refusing to fill my own well; then, I expected obedience from my children as a way of proving that I mattered. This allegiance to a semblance of order wrestled from severely applied discipline led to a prickly atmosphere of unhappy kids. There's a big difference between laying down rules that are based upon foundational values and then instilling the expectation of consistent observance of said rules, and lording your power over your children in order to make yourself feel omnipotent. The former works, and the latter leads to rebellion and an unhappy, tension-filled home.

Making rules that are tied to an outcome that's not based in family values is like buying a gym membership to look good without any thought as to why. New Year's resolutions to work out and look good will fizzle if there's no value-based reason for continuing. Whereas, if you join a gym to meet new people and to immerse yourself in a healthy lifestyle that will add energy and years to your life, then you will be much more likely to keep going. If your rules are about making you feel more respected, they will not help your kids, especially as your kids turn into pre-teens and teenagers. However, if your rules are based upon your family value of showing everyone respect and kindness, regardless of their position, then you don't have to defend them; those rules will stand on their own. When your system of discipline is based upon family values that you believe down to your core, *and* you enforce said system with humor, then your house will be much happier…a place that your kids will want to come home to and bring their friends with them.

If you needed additional reasons you want to run your home with humor, try these: 1) parenting is hard enough without adding the struggle of cramming rules down your children's throats, and 2) preaching that nothing in life is so serious that you can't laugh at it is a beautiful coping mechanism for your kids, especially as they become teenagers. All the parenting tips that work on younger kids are a great foundation for when your kids are thrown into the social mosh pit of middle and high school. But before we talk about the teen years, I want to take you through how to parent when some catalytic event propels you into dealing with change.

Parenting during
Periods of Flux

Introduction to Mastering Change

Accepting and mastering change has helped me navigate the maze of parenting during crises. The basic premise of mastering change is, "just when you think you have it all figured out, everything changes...and that's okay." As parents, we know that our children will grow and change, but no one tells us that our expectations and perceptions need to change as well. We can't support our children in their growth if we are afraid of change ourselves. Martha Beck illustrates the Change Cycle with the life cycle of a butterfly, starting with a caterpillar and ending with a butterfly, in her book *Finding Your Own North Star*. Here's a pictorial version similar to the one that's in the book.

The Basic Change Cycle

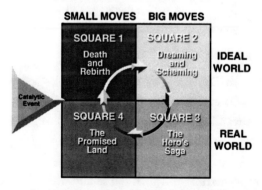

Reprinted with permission. Martha Beck, Inc. copyright 2008

The Change Cycle is a handy illustration of a pattern of growth that exists in nature, and if we can adopt an attitude of acceptance instead of fear, we can teach our kids to prosper during the changes that life is perpetually throwing at us. The beauty part of understanding and working with change in your everyday parenting life is that you can pattern what acceptance of new ideas and situations looks like for your kid. That way when they find out that the girl/sport/guy/instrument they were banking on to make them happy doesn't pan out, this is what you do instead of giving up. The way I use the four squares in my parenting is as follows:

Square One: Starting All Over: This first square in the change cycle is likened to a caterpillar morphing inside the chrysalis to begin its transformation into a butterfly. If you've had a major life change—like divorce, death in the family, or your child going to college—and you have no idea where to go or what to do, then you're in Square One. Most of my clients are in Square One when they hire me. The trick in Square One is that—like the caterpillar that dissolves into goo before it begins to take on the new DNA of the butterfly—you must dissolve your old identity before you can adapt to a new one. This dissolving is accompanied by grief… sometimes, a boatload of grief.

Square Two: Dreaming Up a New You: Once you have grieved the loss of whatever illusions you brought into Square One, you can begin dreaming about who you want to become. If you can't dream it, you can't be it. This is my favorite square, and I return to it often as a respite from the reality of Square Three. This book was born in Square Two. This is the square where the caterpillar dreams of becoming a butterfly. Square One and Square Two both take place internally, inside the chrysalis; to the outside world, you look much the same. However, these internal changes will create the foundation, or the code, for the new butterfly form that is developed in Square Three.

Square Three: Falling Down And Getting Up, And Falling Some More: Once you've grieved the loss of your old life, and then dreamed up a new one, Square Three is how to reach your new vision…one tiny baby step at a time. A baby step is the smallest, most ridiculously easy step you can take with a light and happy heart. For instance, if you want to write a book, maybe a baby step is to find a writing space in your house that feels really good to your Inner Guide. I love to write on my treadmill workstation with the soft lighting of my desk lamp, smooth jazz from Pandora playing, and Gramma's Cookies incense burning. I came up with this Writer's Corner using baby steps: setting my alarm for fifteen minutes a day over the span of a week, while I imagined a space that would be like catnip for my creative muse. Then I proceeded to create that space trying different options. Square Three is a tough square, in that it involves trying and failing over and over again. The butterfly's struggles to free herself from the chrysalis are necessary to strengthen her wings enough to fly. Within Square Three, you will fail and return to Square One many times, each time getting a little bit closer to the implementation of your Square Two vision. When you put together enough baby steps to reach your goal, then you are ready for Square Four.

Square Four: You're in the Groove: Square Four is a wonderful place where small adjustments will keep you sailing along; Square Two and Three are the squares where big shifts happen. Square

Two shifts are internal (dreaming a new life) and Square Three shifts are external (making that new life happen). Like Square One, you don't want to make big decisions or shifts in Square Four, but unlike Square One, the adjustments in Square Four are external… tiny adjustments that make it even better. Because it feels so safe, it's tempting to live in Square Four all the time. However, if you choose to do that, you won't grow. You will stay in your own story about how change is too difficult and scary. I know people who stay in Square Four all of their lives, talking about how their lives will be better when they get a new job, boyfriend, or lose weight, thinking that change must come from outside themselves, when all the while the only lasting change comes from within. And because they don't know how to change, they stay in Square Four, where they are safe but unfulfilled. Or worse, they try to prevent their child from changing, because the thought of Square One is too scary for them. This situation leads to a clinging parent and a rebellious child.

Now, let's look at how the Change Cycle can play out in parenting, both negatively and positively. At every high school reunion, we have encountered the fifty-year-old who insists on staying in high school emotionally, because that's where he was king of the hill (I use "he" without prejudice, it could just as easily be a "she"). Until he lets the identity of high school football stud dissolve (Square One), he will never grow into anything else. This is the guy who either wants to be friends with his kids, because he can capture a little taste of the success he had in high school, or is unreasonably restrictive of his kids, so that they won't grow and change without him. However, *we are not here to be our kids' friend, we are here to be their parent.*

The longer you force your children to stay dependent upon you, or your ideas of what they should be, the worse they will be prepared for an independent life. Remember, our goal is to raise responsible citizens who respect other ways of life while celebrating their own.

So let's take said "stud" through the squares. Like the light bulb encountered by multiple therapists, first he has to *want* to change. If something in his life propels him into Square One, say his high school-aged son comes home one day to tell him that he's gay, then here's what could happen if the dad resists change. His "high school stud with a studly son" identity comes crashing down around him. If he chooses to stay in Square Four, he will kick out his son and blame someone else for his misfortune, perhaps his ex-wife. He will write the "defective stud" out of his life and perhaps turn to alcohol or some other substance to dull his pain. He'll stop taking care of himself; no more early morning workouts to maintain his physique. After all, who cares about what he washes down with the alcohol, bring on the junk food…it doesn't really matter anyway, because his "life is over." He puts on weight, develops heart disease, and dies a lonely old man surrounded by bored young dates.

Now, let's look at what happens if he embraces change. At first he is pissed. How could this happen to him? Didn't he put his son in every lesson for baseball, football, basketball, or really anything with a ball? (Yes, I heard the joke; let's focus). Wasn't he there at every practice, trying to cheer on his son, encouraging him to practice, when all his son wanted was to join the drama, debate, theater, or dance team? (I'm using examples from my daughter's friends.) He knew his son was unhappy, but he just thought he needed to focus.

This anger continues until he realizes that all of those dreams were *his* dreams…not his son's. Since he loves his boy, he moves forward to grieving the demise of his version of his son's success and builds a new way of relating to his son (Square One). Because he's a good dad, he comes out of his grief and turns to his son to ask, "What do we do now? I love you, but I don't know how to support you in your choice." His son gives him some ideas, and he dreams up ways of being a different kind of dad (Square Two). Then he starts down the road of putting that new dad to work (Square Three): he looks at colleges with kick-ass fine arts programs instead of fierce football teams. He talks with a guy he knew in school that has an internship for an up-and-coming designer. He tries a yoga class. He invites his son's boyfriend to dinner. Finally, after a long road of failing and starting over again, he reaches a new groove…a new relationship with his son (Square Four) that is built on truth and trust. And this year, he has a whole new set of stories to tell at his high school reunion…stories that the right people will *want* to listen to, and the ones that are stuck in their own Square Four will run away from. Maybe this new dad will find a new wife, or perhaps see all the things he was blind to with the previous one, and he will live a long and satisfying life, surfing the waves of change as new challenges arise. I can hear some of you shaking your head, saying, "Yeah, right." But I have seen improbably wondrous things happen when my clients start accepting and then riding change into a better life.

To begin mastering change, you must take stock of where you *are* right now, as opposed to where you think you *should* be. I became queen of change because of my aforementioned bad year. I learned that change introduces the most important lesson for bringing more joy into your life…acceptance. As Byron Katie says,

"When you argue with reality, you lose, but only a hundred percent of the time." Accepting that you are exactly where you're supposed to be to learn the lesson you're supposed to learn will allow you to master change. Focusing on the lesson that exists where you are, instead of mourning why you're not where you think you ought to be, is crucial to move forward into the next square. Look at the following list of personality types to see which one resonates with where you are right now. Then we will go through each of the squares to help you move forward to a life that is buoyant and adaptable instead of murky and stuck:

Square 1: Chaos Cravers. People who are fond of Square One are most comfortable in crisis mode. They live on the edge where the next crisis will give them that hit of adrenaline that makes them feel alive. These people feel best when they are cheating a deadline or doing high-adrenaline activities, like extreme sports or riding roller coasters. These are also the drama mamas who are perpetually astounded by how unfair life has treated them and their little princes or princesses. These people may have been raised in a house where the only attention they received was when they were in crisis. Anything less than a four-alarm fire was ignored by their parents. On the plus side, these are also the people that we rely upon in emergencies: the firemen, ambulance drivers, cops, and ER doctors. The tough square for these people is Square Four, where not a lot happens. As a result, they may create chaos just to get back to Square One...just ask all their exes. For these types to be content, they first have to accept who they are and then mold a life that has excitement built in to a path toward lasting goals and relationships.

Square 2: Big Dreamer. People who love Square Two, like me, can dream up amazing new lives in intricate detail, but the actual steps to make that life happen are often too scary to face. These are the people who research a subject ad nauseam before taking an actual step. Square Two people tend to get stuck in "analysis paralysis," forever refining their plans for action without actually taking any steps. On the plus side, we wouldn't have any new technology or art without some Square Two person dreaming it up. Activities that appeal to Square Two people are creative in nature—painting, knitting, crafting, sculpting, and writing. Square Two people tend to need blocks of alone time, or they start to feel stifled and anxious. It's important for me to block out time for meditation on a daily basis, so that my brain can rest from all that dreaming.

Square 3: Human "Do-ing". These people are in perpetual "doing" mode (I used to be like this, as I'm a Square 2/Square 3 hybrid). If you want a party planned or a field trip organized, these are your make-it-happen folks. PTA is filled with Square Three lovers, and they are vital to the success of any endeavor that requires more than one variable to succeed. However, Square Three people are perpetually doing with an outward focus, and they rarely take the time to introspect to see if all that doing is taking them in the right direction. These are "trees" people who rarely pull back to see what the forest looks like. They benefit from some Square Two dreaming time, but they rarely want to stop doing long enough to dream. Square Three people can do moving meditation, like walking, yoga, or dance. The body is moving, but the mind can rest. If they don't build in mental rest time, they can become burned out or sick. Self-care is even more important for Square Three folks than those in other squares.

Square 4: Solid as a Rock. Square Four people are those who have an answer for everything; they do things one way, because that's the way they've always been done. They aren't concerned with new fads or ways of accomplishing new goals. They stay in the same job, house, or relationship for years without even thinking about change, because their scope is so narrow. On the plus side, they are loyal, steadfast, and level-headed. If they are happy in their life, that's fine. But if they feel stifled, it's very difficult for them to jump into Square One to start a new path. A daily practice of gratitude can keep these people from becoming stifled.

After you realize which square your personality resonates with, you can use the activities suited to that square as a kind of self-care. I love Square Two, so I build a little dreaming time into my schedule, especially when I'm in Square Three. I sit down with my journal for ten-to-fifteen minutes of free-hand morning pages on a daily basis. It's amazing what comes up: ideas for blog posts, creative ways to tackle issues, and some gobbledygook that means nothing. The important thing is the respite this Square Two time affords me. It's even better if I can take my journal outside; nature has a calming, energizing effect that is always there for the taking.

All four personality types have their strengths and weaknesses, as well as different ways of approaching change. In the next few chapters, we will explore ways of using your inherent personality type to make the change cycle work for you, so that change becomes more comfortable for you and for your child. I have split each quadrant into different growth stages in your child's development, so that you can see how to make each work best for you and your child, no matter what stage you're both in. Remember, anticipating the next square instead of fighting the change inherent in growth is the only way to build a level of acceptance into your daily life, thereby increasing your parental joy quotient.

CHAPTER TEN

Where Are You Now?
Square One:
Starting all Over

If you have encountered some catalytic event, either external (change in job, relationship, a physical move, or unexpected illness) or internal (you look around and decide that you can't take one more day of living the same old life), and you feel like someone has changed all the rules, you're in Square One. I highly recommend that when you're in Square One, you say to yourself, "I know things seem bleak, but everything will be okay. This is just what Square One looks like." An acceptance of where you are is crucial to moving forward through the squares. The idea that you're exactly where you're supposed to be to learn the lesson you're supposed to learn leads to a more observer-based perspective; the more you can remain in observer mode, without judgment, the better Square One will treat you.

Square One is not the time to make big decisions; it *is* the time to get real comfortable with discomfort. Then, and only then, can you move on to Square Two. Square One hits you in each stage of your child's development. As your child leaves behind one stage, you also need to leave behind the identity that molded with that stage. That way you can support your child in a way that is appropriate for the next stage. If you have multiple children in multiple stages, then you will have multiple identities...and that's okay. Again, accept that Square One can be weird and uncomfortable; feel the discomfort, and it will end a lot faster. If you open your mind to accept change, you won't waste energy trying to stop it. You can instead use that energy to help you and your child move forward. The following are some of the major milestones, and their inherent challenges, that I have observed with my kids and with my clients:

Baby to Toddler: When your baby starts walking, the world changes for both of you; every light socket and small object becomes a threat. Instead of fighting the change, accept this new being and prepare her environment to help her reach her next stage. Each developmental milestone in your kid's life is a brand new Square One for both of you. When you can anticipate the changes, you can better prepare for them. When your baby is napping or finally sleeping through the night, rest yourself. Realize that without a regular sleep cycle, you are not going to be able to do all the things you used to do; ask for help! As I tell all my clients, you don't get points for suffering. You are doing yourself and your child a huge disservice by trying to hold onto a standard of pre-baby efficiency; if you're focused on keeping your life running like a well-oiled machine, then you will miss all the daily magic of having a baby. The first couple of years of your child's life are messy; accept the mess, nay, learn to love the mess. Accept that piles of dirty laundry are par for the course in this stage; you can live in a clean house in some future stage.

The Terrible Twos and Pre-school: This is the stage where your well-mannered baby begins parroting bad behavior that he learns from other pre-schoolers. If you try to force him back to the angel he was when he entered school or pretend that the changes aren't there, you will end up frustrated. Accept the change and work within the new system. This is why choosing a pre-school that agrees with your type of discipline is so important. You want discipline to be consistent throughout your child's day, so that you can just focus upon the socialization challenges that arise from being around other kids who come from parents who may parent differently than you. Self-care is very important in this stage, so that your energy level is high enough to roll with the changes. Put nutritious foods, exercise, and quiet time on your schedule to maintain balance.

Kindergarten/Elementary School: In elementary school, your child will learn how to work within a system, or she will become very well-acquainted with the principal. Your method of discipline and value-based rules will come in handy in this stage. Follow your Body Compass to develop your rules and apply them consistently, regardless of what other parents are doing. The Square One issues in this stage run the gamut from the elimination of naptime (this was huge in our house and led to a couple of weeks of exhausted after-school tantrums) to the frustrations inherent in learning to read and write. The best strategy is to not play the "compare-and-despair" game. When the mouthy mom lets it "slip" that her little Suzie is reading at a high-school level in the first grade, choose not to play. Quell the chant of, "What am I doing wrong? My child is barely reading at all. She's going to flunk first grade, and we will all be shunned!" Like any other Square One issue, the best strategy is to stop and take three deep belly breaths. Quiet the fight-or-flight response by sitting still and focusing on your exhale until you can hear your heartbeat, then breathe in deeply once again. Just three breaths, and then maybe another three breaths, and you will return to the wisdom of your body and the message of your Inner Guide, "All is well."

Middle School: 6th, 7th, and 8th grade is a huge Petri dish of change. Your child is going through puberty and all its inherent physical changes, while at the same time trying to figure out how to navigate the middle school social landscape. It's even more important to stay connected to your child as they react to all these changes. The most common Square One development in middle school is peer pressure. When your sweet lamb of an eleven-year-old starts acting like a teenager, you will be better equipped to handle it if you expect it. This is a good stage to introduce the Inner Guide/Inner Judge balance that is so important to navigate Square One.

All you need to do in middle school is introduce the concept of the two selves, so that your child can recognize how it feels to listen to a group mentality instead of what their inner voice is telling them. Going against your Inner Guide to try to fit into a group that doesn't include *Your People* (people who have the same vision and goals as you) feels bad and icky...a sort of quivery, nauseous feeling. Ask your child to tell you very specifically how this feels in their body; then they will know to avoid the situation or the people around them when that feeling comes up.

If you don't practice this concept yourself, it's nearly impossible to teach it to your child. Take a moment to look at your circle of friends. Are they supportive of your individual goals? Is there an equal give and take to the relationship? Do you gag your Inner Guide in order to blend in? If you're not surrounding yourself with Your People, ask yourself, "Why not?"

For many years, I didn't have any close friends, because I didn't think that open-minded, spirituality seeking, granola types existed in my small Southern town. However, when I used my life coaching tools to find out who I was and what I desired for my life, then I started to embody my Inner Guide. As soon as I started being authentic, My People found me…but it took some time. In life coach training we learned about a phenomenon called "the empty elevator syndrome" on the path to authenticity. Think of yourself on an elevator with your social circle as it exists today. As you go up toward authenticity, you will lose friends who don't match your new level of enlightenment; as you rise to the next floor, they may exit the elevator. That's okay; let them go. That creates space in your life for Your People to get on and continue to ride with you, supporting your journey to your higher self. This space may take a while to fill, which means you could be in an empty elevator for a while. Use this time to work on becoming the best and most authentic version of yourself.

Practice radical self-care and keep marching toward your goals one baby step at a time. I highly recommend doing the same soul searching for yourself when you're setting your Eagle Vision goals for your child. Square One is about letting go of the old you and re-birthing a new version based on your Inner Guide's wisdom. In Square Two you can set Eagle Vision goals for your Guide, then take Mouse Vision steps in Square Three to find Your People to support you. You will not find Your People sitting on your couch.

Break out of your routine and try something different. Take a class that interests you or try a new, funky restaurant that sounds delicious…Your People will be waiting for you.

Once we practice being our authentic selves, then we can help our middle schoolers do the same. We want to encourage our middle schoolers to listen to their own wisdom over the social directive to do anything necessary to fit in. That way they will be projecting an authentic version of themselves in high school, so that kindred souls can find them, thereby shrinking the big pond to a friendly little puddle.

High School: Fasten Your Seat Belts…it's going to be a bumpy ride! When your middle schooler goes to high school, it's the biggest, scariest Square One change of all. Depending upon how your school breaks it up, your ninth or 10th grader will be thrown into the same pot as seventeen- to eighteen-year-old pseudo-adults. If your fourteen- or fifteen-year-old is a pretty, sensitive girl, or a small sensitive boy, it makes it even scarier. I have gone through this particular Square One twice, and it wasn't fun. Then again, I didn't have life coaching tools or the ability to master change back then. The best action we can take as a parent is to do our own work first. (Refer back to Chapter Five for an explanation of Byron Katie's tool, "The Work.") Basically, doing your own work means that you separate how you feel from how your kid feels. If his issues are bringing up your old traumatic memories of being shoved in a gym locker as a freshman, you won't be able to support him effectively.

You must deal with your own stuff first, and then you can help your kids. Be sensitive to the change that your kids are experiencing in high school: the demise of their safe, secure environment where teachers were more hands on, spoon-feeding them their education, and sex and drugs were not an issue (this, of course, depends upon the middle school; some middle schools are like high schools, so adjust this to the previous section). They must then create a high school persona while faced with a plethora of threats and temptations for their Judge to gag any Guide messages. This is where high school can be so damaging to a sensitive soul: kids stop playing in high school and start merely playing a part... and not in a good, creative drama club way. They play the part of "the cool kid" who's not shocked by anything, or even surprised, but who is also not delighted by anything. This sardonic, cool-kid persona stomps creativity and joy under its steel-toed boots, and the sensitive soul starts to wither.

As parents, we need to adjust our expectations of our freshmen with an awareness of all the upheaval they are experiencing on a regular basis. They spend all day with adults talking at them and big kids pulling on them; when they come home, they don't need more of the same. They need someone to listen. If you don't listen, they will find someone else who will...trust me. And if your child doesn't have a strong support group of like-minded kids, they will be ripe for some emotional vampire to suck them dry, all in the guise of being understanding. Freshman year is a time for parents to become Mom and Dad 2.0, with adjusted expectations.

They need to pare down their household rules to a minimum, keeping only the rules that reflect the values and beliefs of the family. In my house, that means I just shut my teenagers' doors when they're gone. I fought with them for years about picking up their rooms, and it was a ridiculously frustrating experience for all of us. I would get furious, clean the rooms myself, and rail at them. One day, I realized this was a *huge* waste of time. So I started shutting the doors. When they can't find that notebook, piece of paper, or "one perfect skirt" they need, I smile and gently remind them that they would know where it was if they put it back (okay, maybe I dance around with glee inside, but my façade is gentle). If you can let the identity and rules of middle school die and rebirth a new high-school parent persona whose ratio of listening to talking is at least 2:1, then you can move on to Square Two and dream up a new relationship with your burgeoning young adult.

CHAPTER ELEVEN

Where Do You Want to Be? Square Two: Dreaming up a New You

Square Two is where you dream up a new you, and you can decide how that looks. There are no hard and fast rules, because you will be making up the rules as you're flying the plane...or some other metaphor that is hopelessly mixed. Square Two is full of big changes, but they're mostly in your head and heart. You have left behind the parent you were in Square One, and this is the square where you can dream up a new version using your Eagle Vision; you are in charge of what that version 2.0 parent will look like. Since Eagle Vision is long term, you can see far into the distance, but the details are fuzzy. That's okay, because the details will become clear in Square Three, where you will become very adept at using Mouse Vision to see your next step. To establish your Eagle Vision goals for your new parental persona, I like to use an exercise called My Best Parenting Day Ever.

This is a dreamy tool that will necessitate that you check your logical self at the door. You can pick him or her back up again when we're finished...I promise. Pick a momentous occasion in your child's future, say high school or college graduation. Imagine that she is standing in front of a microphone making a speech, perhaps because she's been elected valedictorian! In this speech, she thanks you for everything you've done to get her to this historic day. There she stands, your little miracle, making a speech about what it was like to be raised by you. Write this vision down and be very specific about what you want her to say. Put in details of what the scene looks and smells like; use as many sensory details as you can to give it texture and heft. Make sure this feels amazing and light in your body; your chest expands, because your heart is so full of love. Your brain clears, and you feel like you can do anything. That's the feeling state of pure creativity. This state is what Square Two is all about. The challenge for you, and for your child, is to leave logic on the sidelines long enough to let your Square Two dreams run their course. When you've finished dreaming how you want your future relationship with your child to look, then, and only then, can you move beyond Square Two to figure out the individual steps you need to take in Square Three to make this Square Two dream a reality. Now let's go through the stages to see how Square Two looks at different ages.

Baby to Toddler: The application of Square Two in this stage is all about play. I've already mentioned the need to be very comfortable with inefficiency and mess when you have a little one, now I'm going suggest you dream about your ideal day as a mom *in this stage*. Don't focus on what you have to do, think about what you want to do; imagine that you only have this one day with your baby. I bet if you let the chore side of being a mom fall away, you might structure your day a bit differently. For me, this meant getting help with the laundry, so that I could read to my kids, play blocks with them, and sing and dance with them. Nothing is more important than playing with your kids at this stage; it makes them feel secure, and it makes you feel like a better version of yourself. Even if you are faced with leaving your baby at daycare because your household needs your income, you can still stop and play for fifteen to thirty minutes when you pick him up. Take the time you would normally watch TV and spend it doing something playful with your child. Spend a little time in creative play every day to become a better parent and a happier person.

The Terrible Twos and Pre-School: This stage is very similar to the last as it pertains to Square Two actions. Again, focus on play whenever you can. This is the stage where you may be tempted to buy lots of toys for your kids to make up for not being there, if your job requires long hours away from your family. Resist that temptation. Instead, take the time to play with your kids using the toys they already have. When your pre-schooler sits down to color, pull up a chair and a crayon yourself. This will show your child that you are with them emotionally as well as physically; this is the perfect time to start a lifelong bond with your child built upon creativity instead of stuff. It will teach her to value connection over material things…experience over consumption. You think that you need a drink and a spell in front of reality television to escape, but there is no better escape than finger-paints, paper, and your little artist at your elbow…and the beauty part is that when you choose creative play, you can actually remember and cherish what happened. This is Plugged-In Parenting. You can do this; it's your choice. Try unplugging the television and computer for a day and pretend that you're living in pre-media times; make it a game for you and your child. I highly doubt many people are laying on their deathbeds wishing they had worked or vegged out one more day.

Kindergarten/Elementary School: In kindergarten, school is play-based, so home can be an extension of what your child is experiencing in school. It doesn't take a lot of time to make your child feel important, a little goes a long way. The rule that homework is done right after the kids arrive home opens up a time when you can do household chores and still interact with your kids while they do homework. Ask them about school while you're folding clothes or doing the dishes. After homework's finished, you can both chat while they help make dinner. Better yet, crank some tunes while you're doing chores with your kids...music makes everything better. Keep that Eagle Vision ideal day in the back of your head, and structure your Mouse Vision day to support a road to that dream. Would your valedictorian be thanking you for your support if you parked them in front of a video while you were on Facebook? You think that surfing the net is restful downtime, but do you feel rested afterward? I don't. I feel keyed up, like I have an itch I can't scratch. I'm not knocking Facebook; it can be a wonderful tool for connecting to Your People who don't live near you. I keep in contact with my tribe of coaching buddies with Facebook, but I don't spend my precious Mommy time just cruising other people's lives without purpose; my daughters call this Facebook stalking. If you use social media to always entertain yourself instead of playing with your kids, that future day will look much different. Elementary school is where your kids develop dreams of who they want to be when they grow up; you want to be a part of that dreaming process.

That way you can help to refocus them on what is important when middle and high school threaten to quash those dreams.

Middle School: In our district, middle school is the first time that kids change classes like high school kids, try out for sports teams like high school kids, and go to dances like high school kids. Middle school is the Square Two version of high school. Your child can dream up the person he or she will be in high school without all the pressures of drugs, sex, and cliques that come with high school (again, this depends upon your middle school). Intrinsic in this dreaming is a dress rehearsal of their new persona; then they can figure out if it fits or whether it needs to be tossed for another one. Middle school is where your child should pick up that new instrument, sport, chorus, or theater class they've always wanted to try. They may find a new inspiration and group of friends that will carry them through high school without a hitch. For my two oldest girls, this group was cheerleading. However, they didn't want to carry on with cheerleading in high school, because neither one of them was especially gifted in tumbling. Also, I wasn't nearly as thrilled about them doing stunts on a high school level. Did you know that cheerleading is one of the most dangerous sports your kids can play? (Although my husband insists that it's not a sport, because there's no offense and defense, I think those tiny uniforms are plenty offensive.) For my youngest girl, middle school was all about volleyball. She tried out for the team on a whim and made the developmental squad in sixth grade. At the end of her sixth grade year, she was asked to play with the varsity team in the final tournament of the year. I thought my husband was going to burst with pride. I am hoping that this volleyball persona will carry her through high school, allowing her to float above the emotional vampires that tried to suck her sisters dry. A kid who is busy with something they love has much less time to get involved in actions that don't line up with their Square Two persona.

High School: Square Two in high school is often left in the dust because of pressing Square Three matters like: 1) How do I find my locker? 2) How do I find my next class? 3) How can I get to my locker between classes when the halls are like L.A. rush-hour traffic? (Sidenote: I once painted my nails, two coats plus topcoat, in L.A. rush hour stop-and-stop traffic without a smear or bump. This has no real pertinence to the discussion, I just thought it was weird; or maybe I'm just weird...back to high school). This is why it's so important for your kids to develop their high school persona in middle school and surround themselves with like-minded individuals. They can always change their mind if it doesn't work out, but if they find people who think like them, whether in a club, sport, or art activity like drama or forensics, they don't have to reinvent themselves *and* figure out all the Square Three stuff at the same time. I remember an instance when my middle child was crying because the "popular kids" didn't want to sit with her in the lunchroom (this is why teen movies keep using this scene...because it's really true). She spent so much time worrying about how she was going to make them like her...what she could change about herself so that she would fit in. After days (which felt like years) of hearing this same rant, I asked her, "If you could choose anyone at the school to hang out with, would *you* choose *them*?" After she hemmed and hawed about how popular they were, I asked her the same question. She finally admitted that she didn't really like how they treated other people; she didn't like what they stood for. And I replied, "Then why would you want to hang with them anyway? They aren't Your People! And if you keep hanging with them, Your People will never find you. You have to be exactly who you are if you want Your People to find you. It might not be today or tomorrow, but if you practice being the best YOU, they will show up." It took another couple of years of me saying the same thing over and over for her to believe it, but she gets it now…and she's only twenty! It took me forty years to learn the same lesson.

I became a Square Two lover when I was little. Because both of my parents were Square One drama-holics, I spent a lot of time there by proxy. My only escape was Square Two. I could disappear into my imagination and dream about a family that didn't value drama above love. Since I was little and had no control, I couldn't move forward into Square Three; but I could stay in Square Two and make it beautiful, wonderful, and safe. The most important lesson in Square Two, whether it's happening to you or your child, is to let it play through. You can't rush Square Two, or you will land smack dab in overwhelm. Square Two is built upon an internal landscape, and it's fragile. If you try to push forward to Square Three action too soon, you will go right back to Square One. However, since you didn't finish your dreamtime, you won't know which direction to try next. Each of the squares has its own timeline. You'll know when you're finished with Square One when you start feeling hopeful and new ideas start popping into your head. You'll know you're finished with Square Two when your ideas slow down to a trickle, kind of like listening to the popping of microwave popcorn. When the popping slows considerably, it's time to move to Square Three. If you wait until there's no more popping, you'll burn your popcorn; staying in Square Two too long will lead to analysis paralysis. You will be stuck refining and polishing your dreams, without actually doing anything to make them come true.

If you really enjoy Square Two, like I do, you can use it as a kind of vacation from Square Three. I spend time in Square Two to recharge. I let my imagination run wild, thinking up new ways to bring more joy into my life and the lives of my family. There's no hard and fast rule for when Square Two is finished, but if you plug into your Inner Guide and let it point the way, you will know when it's time for action. When you start to feel antsy in Square Two, then it's time to move forward into the Hero's Saga. Gird your loins; here comes Square Three!

CHAPTER TWELVE

How Do You Get There? Square Three: Falling Down and Getting Up, and Falling Down Some More

Now that you're finished dreaming up how you want your new life to look and feel, complete with a new kind of relationship with your kids and your Inner Guide, Square Three is where you take a lot of little baby steps to move you ever closer to that dream. Baby steps are the answer to "How do you eat an elephant?" (It's one bite at a time, but you knew that). Remember, a baby step is the most ridiculously easy step you can take in a direction that feels joyful. When you come up with a desired goal, then work your way backward to certain milestones necessary to reach that goal. Then you fill in the baby steps that go into making those milestones. If you don't know what steps to fill in down the line, don't worry; if you just keep moving along, the steps will materialize as you gather more information. Once you have worked your way back to where you are today, then you have a very workable plan to reach *any* goal; that includes writing a parenting book!

The beauty of baby steps is that they work so well. If you jump into Square Three trying to make huge strides in the direction of your new dream, you will either burn out or land in the place where it's hard to back up once you've discovered that the direction is not the right one. You will have invested so much, that you can't bear the thought of turning around. With baby steps, you use your Mouse Vision to move forward, while rising up to Eagle Vision every once and awhile to make sure you're still on the right path.

If your dream is to bring art into the relationship with your child, and you jump in feet first, clearing the shelves of your local craft store, then you will feel compelled to push the agenda with your child. Since you've spent so much on art supplies, you want to get your money's worth. So you pressure your child to stay home when she really wants to be with her friends; you turn your dining room into an artist's studio, and now there's no place to eat dinner; you take to wearing an artist's smock and a beret whenever you're home just to "remind" your child how important this is to your relationship…how creative does this feel? Not! It feels heavy and needy, and now you're wearing a smock! You took too big a step.

A baby step would have been to notice what already fascinates your child. My fourteen-year-old is into nail art. She paints the most amazing designs and colors on her nails; my baby step was to offer to be her canvas (see…ridiculously easy! All I had to do was sit there). While she was painting my nails, we talked about why she likes to paint and what other crafts we might try together. This may not have worked; she may have wanted to paint her own nails. So, then I would have tried something else. Square Three is all about trying and failing: going back to Square One, dreaming a new path, and trying again. So let's see how this plays out in the different stages:

Baby to Toddler: After letting go of your idea of the perfect house and family, then spending time on the Square Two playground, the Square Three part of this stage is making life as easy on yourself and your child as possible. Take small steps to baby proof your house. Get down on the floor and see things from your toddler's perspective when you are looking for possible dangers. Put the plastic stoppers in the electric sockets, and put all cherished knick-knacks out of reach. It doesn't matter if your visitors have to deal with latches on cabinets; you're not going to be giving a whole lot of gala events at this stage anyway. (Since I had my first two kids two years apart, the latches stayed on the cabinets for a long time. In fact, it was only a few months after spending hours taking them off that we decided to get pregnant again...oh the irony! So, we got the new-fangled latches, and I continued to break fingernails trying to open cabinets for another three or four years.)

Orient your life around your child's basic developmental needs, and then add in favorite treats for yourself; fold clothes while watching trashy television, take a candlelit bath while your baby sleeps, take your toddler out with you for a stroll. You only get one chance at your baby being a baby; take advantage of the wonder of it. One of my favorite ways to teach language to my babies was to describe everything I was doing; sometimes I would sing it. Like, "I'm changing your diaper, so you're nice and clean," or "Now we're going to put on your shirt and pants. Look how cute you are." My kids all talked very early, and I'm convinced it was because of this little trick. Use Square Three to streamline your child's environment, so that you can connect with your child on a level that is more than just caretaking. If the environment is well baby-proofed, regardless of how it looks, you will have less time cleaning up messes and more time playing with your bundle of joy.

The Terrible Twos and Pre-School: In our house, we had the Terrible Eighteen Months instead of the Terrible Twos. By age two, the temper tantrums had calmed down, in large part due to me strapping on my armor every time I left the house. The courage part of this stage consists of being strong when your pre-schooler tries to exert their new sense of self by defying your rules. Again, "no" means "no". I already introduced this concept at length in Chapter Seven, but it's important enough to mention again. My friend Corinne at my favorite place on earth, Lake Austin Spa Resort[18], says, "You can't live 'no' if you don't say, 'No.'" If you don't teach your kids the value of saying 'no,' then how can they be comfortable using it when faced with a moral dilemma or an emotional vampire?

If you give in on the little battles like, "Mommy, can I have this cereal? I saw it on TV!" when that cereal's only redeeming quality is the amount of money the makers paid the marketing people to make it look like real food, then the big battles like curfews, drinking, and bad behavior are much harder to win. This is the stage to establish a routine of discipline with little problems that will carry you through the big problems in middle school and high school. If you plan ahead for trips to the grocery store by

---

18 www.lakeaustin.com

establishing a routine and saying things, like "If you are very good and help Mommy put food in the cart without whining, we will buy you a treat when we check out," then trips into the public domain become easier. I always packed books or coloring books in the cart next to my little shoppers to keep them distracted. We also played the alphabet game and "I Spy" with products on the shelves.

If you take your kids out to a restaurant, and they act up, take them and your food to go. You have to be willing to follow through on a promise (threat) to take them home if they misbehave. In extreme circumstances, this may mean that you take your screaming child and your groceries to customer service and leave the cart there (you can try to leave the kid, but I don't think the customer service rep will take her). The Square Three issue in this stage is how to keep your discipline consistent. If you set a consequence for bad behavior, make sure it's one that you can act upon. Don't threaten a consequence that you can't deliver in public, because the consequence needs to come swiftly after the bad behavior, in order for the punishment to be meaningful. If your kids are tired and cranky, and your consequence is to go home, then go home; it's likely that things will get worse instead of better if you don't. Every time you follow a bad behavior with a consequence, then you have a reference point for future tussles, and it makes the next struggle easier.

Kindergarten/Elementary School: The best strategy through elementary school is to stay involved, so that you can nip problems in the bud. Develop a relationship with your kid's teacher, so you know what's happening day-to-day. My other strategy is to promote reading in grade school over television. I do this by reading for fun myself. You can't make your kid like to read, but you can set the example that it's a great leisure activity. They don't need to know how much it will help them with writing and speaking in their future. The more they read, the quicker they will pick up the love of language. It will also give you something current to talk to your child about; it's even better if you're both reading the same book…this gives your child the feeling that he carries you around with him in school. I went one step further and volunteered in my child's classroom to help with reading. This is great when they're in first, second, and third grade, then my husband taught a volunteer Sunshine Math program in fourth and fifth grade.

Your presence in the classroom is a big feather in your kid's cap, especially if you actually like kids and can make them laugh. You will be the funny, cool Mrs. Fedonczak. Actually, you won't be Mrs. Fedonczak; that's my job, but you get the picture. Volunteering has the added benefit of your child's friends knowing who you are. When it comes time for that play date or sleepover, they can tell their parents, "Emily's mom volunteers in school. She's really nice." It will give their parents peace of mind. If their parents don't care, that's also good information. Parents who aren't invested in their child's care often spin off children that you may end up banning from your child's life. It's equally as likely that you will be a stabilizing influence in their lives, and your house will become the home they never had. I tell my kids, "If you make friends who have a crummy home life, they are on a different level than you. You can either bring them up to your level, or they can bring you down to theirs. I will be the judge of this. If I see you slipping, I will end things, because that's my job. I won't be mad at them or you. They just won't be invited back. If you pull them up, then I will be happy to have them over as much as you both want." That's how we got our bonus child; she realized that she wanted a different life for herself, and we helped her get there.

Middle School: The Square Three challenge of middle school is to remain flexible and connected: flexible enough to adapt your rules to your child's changing environment and connected enough to know when that environment is changing and your rules should as well. Again, you want to keep your rules wedded to your family values. As your kids make their way through puberty and all its challenges, drop those rules that seem superfluous. I stay connected with my kids through the aforementioned lunch notes as well as our family dinners. Refer back to Chapter Nine on why you want to make your house the place to hang out in Middle School. If you can keep your kids and their approved friends at your house, then the connection becomes much easier.

High School: The Square Three challenge in high school is to know when to step in and fight for your kids; the irony is that sometimes the person you're fighting *is* your kid. What if I have given my high school freshman all the support and love that I can, and she still falls in with a bad crowd and stops talking to me? Freshman year of high school can be really challenging (translation: it really sucks!). I told you this is the biggest Square One of all, and sometimes they just freak out. That doesn't mean *you* have to freak out. It does mean that there may be a point in time that you will need to go to battle stations. This is what happened to me.

When my eldest child began having difficulty in ninth grade, I was flummoxed. She was, and always has been, The Golden

Child (this is her term, not mine. She uses it with her tongue firmly implanted in her cheek). She is the kid everyone wants for their very own…brainy, beautiful, Captain of the Middle School Cheerleaders, and winner of the Math Student of the Year. She never gave me a moment's trouble from birth, and then along comes freshman year…and an alien took possession of my perfect child. Well, an alien and social media. When her behavior began to change, and her grades started slipping, my response was to push her harder. I thought she would snap out of it…wrong! One night, I received a call from a friend that my daughter had posted dubious pictures on her MySpace page, and anyone could see them who had a computer and her name. "OMG! WTF!" My husband and I said these and many other unprintable things when we logged on to see our little angel pouting like a pinup on the Internet.

When I stopped wailing with disbelief, I took ten minutes to breathe and devise an action plan with my spouse. His plan was to lock her in her room until she was thirty-five after taking away anything with an on/off switch. Mine was a little more realistic. First, I sat down with her one-on-one and told her how inappropriate and dangerous her actions were. She at first defended her actions by saying, "We were just playing around, Mom! We weren't seriously trying to be sexy or anything, and we didn't even show anything. God, you are so overreacting!" I responded by bawling. I was so mad and disappointed, not only by her actions, but by her inability to see how destructive they were, that I just lost it. When she saw me crying, she stopped. It finally hit her that what she had done was more than just playing around. She put herself in a position for any pervert on the Web to try to take advantage of her, all in the name of trying to be cool and edgy. I shut down her MySpace page immediately (she told me she thought she had it privacy protected, but she forgot to double-check. These are not the actions of a person with a fully formed frontal lobe).

And then things got worse instead of better. She just stopped talking to me altogether. Her grades went down further (my straight-A student was barely holding onto Bs), and when she looked at me, it was from sullen eyes and a lower lip that you could perch a house upon. As the school year was drawing to a close, I went to battle stations. Since I couldn't seem to reach her or control her environment, I pulled her out of it. As I was in the process of pulling her out of her high school, she won a model search. We embarked upon an adventure of online school and part-time modeling. If the modeling hadn't come along, however, I was going to put her in a charter school to get her away from the emotional vampires that she refused to leave on her own. These were kids that were lost, and they clung to my daughter for her light. Instead of her pulling them up, they pulled her down into their darkness.

Your job as a parent is to do anything within your power to ensure your kids' safety. Once you get him away from whatever it is that is corroding his ability to make good choices, then you can approach building back the relationship you have lost. First, you have to stop the bleeding, and then you can worry about healing the scars. It took a long time to heal those scars. We traveled for two years together, back and forth to New York, sometimes laughing and sometimes fighting, but the travel healed whatever had caused her attraction to darkness. She saw what could be… if she maintained good grades and worked hard. She fell in love with New York City and worked her butt off to get into NYU. She is now back to Golden Child status, a cum laude graduate from NYU, and the world is her oyster again. The bad news is that the same freaking thing happened with her sister.

The second time around, I went to battle stations a lot sooner. My middle child spent most of her freshman year being grounded. When that didn't work, I pulled her out of school kicking and screaming and sent her to a different school before anything life-altering happened. The new school had a different atmosphere that was more centered on the arts than cliques and partying. She went back to her love of singing and developed a different focus. It wasn't easy, and it wasn't quick, but she did come back to us. And today she is thanking me for it. I'm not kidding; she really thanked me. It took a long time, as Square Three often does, but she is now in college with an attitude based in confidence. She's excited about a new challenge, and that makes me very happy. Gone are my middle-of-the-night wake ups, wondering how to get through the belligerent façade; now it's long-distance texts and phone calls for advice and short-distance hugs and smiles. You'll know when Square Three is finished, because things just get easier. You and your kids are in a groove; you start singing in the car on the way to work. Your life feels lighter and more effortless. It's time for Square Four.

CHAPTER THIRTEEN

You've Arrived, Now Be Grateful! Square Four: In the Groove

Square Four is where all your hard work has paid off: the infant is sleeping through the night, and the toddler is potty trained; no more diaper bag! The child can read and write. She has made the basketball team/chess team/debate team...now what? We are back to small changes to maintain balance, until the next catalytic event comes along. Expecting Square One, instead of dreading it, is the key to prospering in Square Four. You can stop looking over your shoulder waiting for something to ripple your placid Square Four lake; you know it's coming, and you know you can handle it when it arrives...because you've done it before. Accept your Square Four success, and be grateful for the results of your hard work; just make tiny adjustments to maintain your balance. A practice of gratitude is important in Square Four. I ask all parents to make teaching gratitude a priority. However, you can't teach gratitude if you don't practice it yourself. Refer back to Chapter One for tips on establishing a gratitude practice.

Gratitude is the only antidote to a sense of, "What's next, and what will I do about it?" When things are good, the old lack-and-attack "caveman brain" is forever whispering about how this won't last…and then what will you do? The "what will I do?" thought comes from a place of fear and lack…fear of the next famine, whether or not a famine actually exists. That is our lizard brain trying to keep ahead of the famine curve. The lizard, or reptilian brain, is the oldest layer in evolutionary terms, so its power over brain function is fundamental.[19] It focuses on lack and attack; it sings the tune of "I don't have enough, and I have to defend myself from harm." It whispers that if you don't have enough (love, youth, shoes, designer outfits, or machines that start with a little i) then you can't be happy. Martha Beck says that fear and gratitude cannot co-exist, so when you're feeling fear, choose gratitude instead. Sit down and write your list of ten things for which you are grateful. Better yet, sit down with your kids and write your lists together. Then look at your list to appreciate how full your life is; use that full, complete feeling to quiet your inner lizard. I often tell my lizard to go lie in the sun and eat a grape; when I need her to look out for danger, I'll let her know. The act of writing my gratitude list brightens my day every single time I do it, and it's much more reliable and less expensive than shopping for new shoes. (I now incorporate my gratitude lists into my morning pages. Before I close down my pages, I write my list of ten things. If I'm having a crappy morning, I start my pages with the list.) The Heartmath method[20] is very similar to using a gratitude list, except it's quicker and you don't need pen and paper.

---

19 thebrain.mcgill.ca/index.php This website gives you a very easy to understand schematic of the brain and its functions. You can choose the level of complexity in the explanations, so that you can explain the functions in terms that your older child will understand.
20 www.heartmath.com

I used this method to conquer an omnipresent case of road rage. The Heartmath method teaches you to deal with stress in the moment, not wait until "you have time." This is crucial for maintaining balance in Square Four. Old wolf-baby habits can flip you into a Square One dilemma without any change in circumstances to warrant it. If you can practice this method in typically stressful times, such as driving in traffic behind rubbernecking tourists when you're late for an appointment, then you can choose acceptance over anxiety. The way I apply the method is to think of a scene that brings me great joy; I use rocking my youngest when she was a baby. My rocking chair was by the window, and her nap coincided with a time in the afternoon when the sun would turn her room golden and warm. I could rock her and watch the ripples on the bayou outside, with the occasional osprey flying by with his dinner in his beak. I put myself back in that rocking chair, smelling the inimitable aroma of fresh baby, feeling her breath against my neck, hearing her sigh of contentment, and watching the afternoon light dance around the room. The more senses you can bring to the party the better. Then just be there, in that moment, and feel your body relax, your heart-rate drop, your shoulders come out of your ears... it's magical. It takes practice, but before long, you can quiet your mind in less than thirty seconds. If you teach your children to use gratitude to combat fear (you can both buy your gratitude/morning pages journals together...make it a special outing) and use a visualization technique like Heartmath to quiet their mind during stressful situations, you will all be happier and better suited to life without an on/off switch. Now let's go through the Square-Four stages:

Baby to Toddler: In this stage, it's helpful to remember that Square Four is fleeting. Just when your baby starts sleeping through the night, he starts teething…and there goes the contentment bubble. If you are prepared for the fact that Square Four has an ever-changing landscape, it won't hit you so hard when the terrain becomes less tranquil. I remember being in an airport chasing my toddler around while I had a baby in a backpack. A grey-haired grandpa caught my eye and smiled while remarking, "You spend the first year encouraging them to walk and talk and the next seventeen years telling them to sit down and be quiet" Yup, that's about right. If you can accept the intransigence of the quiet times, you can laugh at the chaos when it comes around again. I have always referred to our house as a three-ring circus with me wearing the top hat, and I love it. It's a little tame with only one girl still at home; perhaps I'll get a tiger to train?

The Terrible Twos and Pre-School: This stage is also filled with circular, back-to-Square-One movement. Like a WWII Brit, it's best to "Keep Calm and Carry On." If you approach each new challenge with calm and acceptance, you can dial the change dial back to Square Four a lot quicker. I also highly recommend developing a sense of humor; some stuff is just too crazy not to laugh at. In fact the crazier it gets, the bigger the laughter. When my eldest was about eighteen months old, she threw a temper tantrum in the kitchen; she was screaming and stomping her feet, and normally I would have ignored her. This had been a bad day, and I just couldn't take it anymore. I was washing dishes, and I turned around and squirted her with the spray nozzle. It shocked us both so much that we started laughing. I wouldn't advocate this as a form of discipline on a regular basis; however, it didn't hurt her, and it did solve the problem. Another of my basic discipline tenets is, "Do whatever works." If you are flexible and willing to think outside the box while still maintaining a basic structure of discipline, you can create your own normal that leaves you and your kids feeling secure and loved.

Kindergarten/Elementary School: Once your child starts having homework, it's a great practice for you to establish a routine that your child can use throughout their academic journey. Square Four is the place to create systems that work. You have been through the trials of the other squares, and now you are sailing along. This is the time to look at your schedules and other systems to streamline while you have time and energy. When the next catalytic event comes along, it will be easier to get back to Square Four with your system already in place. You won't be floundering and wondering what to do.

- For instance, establishing a before- and after-school routine is crucial. Before bed, you and your child pick out tomorrow's clothes, check to make sure backpacks are ready to go, and notes are signed. That way the breakfast flows along without chaos; then your child goes to school calm instead of rattled by a chaotic morning. All you have to do is wake them up, feed them, and scoot them out the door. Speaking of feeding them, you do make breakfast, right? Breakfast is a great way to connect with your child one-on-one, or in our house until very recently, one-on-three. I am a big proponent of green smoothies, and we share them at breakfast, along with scrambled egg whites and some form of whole wheat bread. I make the smoothies the night before and then put them in a big thermos in the fridge. That way, even if they barter away all the healthy food I've put in their lunchbox, they have still had antioxidants and protein for breakfast.

- After you set your morning routine, you also develop an after-school schedule that involves a snack, and then they immediately sit down to homework. When homework is finished, your child shows you the assignment list, or calls the Homework Hotline to make sure she has everything completed. This is establishing good habits for middle and high school. If this sounds like a lot, that's because it is. This is why your self–care is so important, so that all the organization and scheduling that is so comforting for your child doesn't make you want to hit your head against a wall.

Middle School: The Square Four priority in Middle School is to come up with your list of priorities. You have pared down your rules to ones that are important to your family values, and you're being flexible about the rest. Now it's time to look at your priorities during the school week. As I've already said, our house rule is to do homework as soon as the kids arrive home. I've tried other methods, but it works best for our family to finish homework while the kids are still in school mode. When homework is finished, then they can play and chat with their friends. We also do homework around our dining room table, so that an adult is there for support if things go wrong. Even if you are In the Groove with your pre-teen communication skills, middle school subjects can go very wrong, very fast. The balance between social demands and academic needs is an ever-changing landscape in middle school, and the way you handle it will set up how you deal with the bigger high school issues.

- In our house it was Math Wars. My brilliant little one had a year-long hiccup with algebra. It was her first B, and at one point she slipped to a C. It wasn't that she wasn't smart enough or didn't work hard enough, there was a real disconnect in how she comprehended the math. We had a similar problem in elementary school, but the math wasn't so hard that she couldn't fake it. Algebra was a whole new world. She kept pooh-poohing my concerns, saying that she had it now; then she would bring home another B or C on a test. Before hiring a tutor, we discovered the Khan Academy[21]. If your kids are having trouble in school, I highly recommend checking out www.khanacademy.org; my daughter's algebra grades are living proof that it works!

Since I was a little preoccupied with my aforementioned awful year, we didn't recover my daughter's A in math, but she did finish the year with an 89, B…or as we like to call it, the most frustrating grade in the world! This is a lesson in stepping in when you feel that things are going bad; don't wait for them to get worse.

High School: In our house, there wasn't a lot of Square Four in high school. It was a whole lot of the other squares, but it wasn't until senior year after college applications were finished that I felt like we really hit Square Four. I know other parents who seemed

---

21 You can watch the TEDtalk where Salman Khan explains his program of providing education to any kid who has a computer at this link: www.ted.com/talks/salman_khan_let_s_use_video_to_reinvent_education.html

to have it all together (remember it doesn't help to compare and despair, even though it's difficult not to in high school; I'm talking to myself as much as I'm talking to you), but high school was the biggest, baddest challenge that I've ever experienced. It was worse for me than losing my mom, dad, and breast cancer all rolled into one, because it wasn't happening to me. My kids were hurting and acting like aliens, and I couldn't make it stop. And that's the biggest lesson of all in Square Four: acceptance.

- Even if you feel like you have the world by the tail in your Groove, Square One is coming…it always does. Accepting where you are and the intrinsic qualities of the square you are in is the only way to get to Square Four. If I had accepted the alien as she was at the time, I still could have chosen the same actions of pulling her out of the environment I couldn't change; however, the stress level would have been infinitely lower. When you practice acceptance, and the cornerstone of that practice is a daily gratitude check-in, then you can approach the Square One trauma with a creative puzzle cracker's vision[22]. I like to use the term puzzle cracking instead of problem solving, because it makes better use of your creative brain. When you look at a problem not as something to attack or solve (that feels so heavy…it makes me want to hide in bed under my covers), but as a puzzle to crack, you can get to a solution a heck of a lot faster. Problem solving makes me tired, but I can puzzle crack until the cows came home. This attitude shift has helped me immeasurably with my

---

22 Martha Beck talks about the difference between problem solving and puzzle cracking in her book, *Finding Your Way in a Wild New World*.

outlook on challenges. Having this puzzle-cracking tool in your belt is crucial to maintaining balance in Square Four.

- The other helpful practice in high school is establishing routines on curfews and "whereabouts checks." As I've said in past chapters, our rule in high school when my kids were out with their friends and changed locations, was that they had to text me the address and the last name of the parents. I knew another mom who had her girls take a picture of the front door while she was on the phone, to prove where they were. I never went that far, because it felt icky to my Body Compass. I told my girls, "I trust you, but if I haven't heard from you, I need an address to find you. If you stay in contact with me by text, I won't have to come and find you. There is no greater suffering than not knowing where your child is or if they're hurt. I love you, and you love me; people who love each other care enough to keep communication lines open."

- We also practiced what we preached in the curfew department. We picked a reasonable hour based on the county requirements, and then we stuck to it. If my kids were five minutes late, they experienced consequences. We spent a lot of time staring at pouty, grounded faces, but they eventually adjusted their fun and planned ahead, so that they could make it home in time for curfew. When you can use creative energy to crack a Square One puzzle, like, oh, I don't know, your kid calls you from a party where other kids are making poor choices, and your kid doesn't have a way home and doesn't know what to do;

then you can skip the teeth gnashing and jump right to dreaming up a solution and then acting on it: "I'll be there in fifteen minutes. I will park down the block and text you when I'm there. Just leave quietly; they won't care, and they may not even notice." I know where to go, because we have already established our whereabouts routine. I have one more kid to send through the high school stage. I have high hopes that there will be lots of Square Four time with her, because I now have tools to get her there. I have had great success with my post high school girls using these tools, and I'm chomping at the bit to try them out on my ninth grader. I talk more about my suggestions for coping with teenage issues in the next section.

Now that we have gone through the stages, I bet you're wondering how mastering change looks on a day-to-day basis; I have an example that came up on a family vacation. It was my eldest daughter's 21st birthday, and I had knitted her a scarf as a present. We gave her other presents, but this one was just from me. I had worked on this scarf every day for over a month, and I was very excited about giving it to her... to show her how much I loved her. To give you a bit of background, she thinks my knitting is, well, kind of ridiculous. She is not much of a contemplative, meditative person; she's more of a logical, get-things-done kind of chick. So she doesn't really get how therapeutic knitting is for me. If my foresight was as clear as my hindsight, I might have picked a different gift. But, as usual, I forged ahead, leading with my heart, right into a brick wall. When I gave her the scarf, it was just the two of us, and her reaction was not what I expected. She smiled politely, said how pretty it was, and "thank you"…a thank you that carried the same level of enthusiasm as describing a blind date as "having a great personality."

I was crushed. I had put so much heart and soul into that damn scarf, and all she could say was "thanks, Mom" and give me a lukewarm smile. How dare she! It was about here that I left the room to be alone; the strength of my reaction was a clue that this wasn't about her at all…it was about me. I realized that, once again, I had an expectation of how the moment would play out, instead of just accepting the way it was. I also realized that instead of letting this ruin my day and pouting about it, I needed to let the Change Cycle do its cleansing work.

Square One: I had to grieve the loss of the reaction I had wanted Kinsey to have to my gift. When I allowed the grief to come instead of telling myself how silly I was being, it was over in a few minutes. Then I started all over to figure out what I needed.

Square Two: I dreamed up a way to get over this feeling of being kicked in the stomach. First, I felt the feeling. Then I dreamed up a way past it; I would go to someone else to get the reaction I wanted from Kinsey.

Square Three: I knew I needed to have someone safe to bear witness to my pain, so I called my two eighteen-year-olds into my room and told them what happened; not as a way to tattle on Kinsey, but as a way to work through my disappointment. This was a risky thing to do, as they could have given me the, "Oh Mom, you're just being silly" response, which would have started a whole new cycle of grief. Square Three is fraught with the possibility of things going wrong; but when you are very specific in asking for what you want, your chances are much better for success. So I asked my middle girls for a group hug. I said my feelings were hurt, but it was about me, not Kinsey. And I just needed a little love to salve my wounds. They were so kind; they hugged me and said they understood. They even related something nice that Kinsey had told them about the scarf, which made me feel better. So I got exactly what I asked for, so on to…

Square Four: The next step was to relax and accept the success. I let it go. This is the hardest part of Square Four—just accepting the success without trying to tweak it. When I let it go, Kinsey came around to a more loving and gracious state of mind. Not because I told her to or guilted her into it, but just because my satisfied energy allowed it.

Since I didn't continue to polish my Square One pain, like Gollum polished his "precious" in Lord of the Rings, Kinsey didn't feel the need to carry on her "cool kid" demeanor. And the whole thing was accomplished in about twenty minutes. This is the beauty of mastering change. When you recognize that you are holding onto something that makes you feel crummy, change it: 1) Stop and figure out where you need to grieve a loss, 2) Dream up a solution, 3) Have the courage to be vulnerable enough to try a new approach, and then, 4) Accept the result. And that's it, folks, you are now the Change Master!

Now let's take a look at the Teen Years.

Parenting Tweens and Teens and Writing Your Own Plan

CHAPTER FOURTEEN

Disciplining Older Kids

As I've said in previous chapters, when your kids reach the teen years, they will react differently to discipline. The teen years are where a sense of humor is your most important parenting tool. Parenting teens is akin to dealing with an attack dog; don't show fear or doubt, or they will eat you alive. Wait, let me rephrase that; if you have fear and doubt and you try to fake a sense of certainty or use an I-know-it-all-and-you-know-nothing attitude, *then* they will eat you alive. If, however, you express your fears and doubts honestly and approach your teens with an open dialogue, then the results will be much less harmful to all involved. If you are honest with them, they won't eat you alive or dismiss you; they might even ignore their knee-jerk disdain and actually engage in a dialogue with you.

As long as they're talking to you, you haven't lost them. If you don't have teens yet, there is a very good chance that the teen years will change your baby into some strange being you don't recognize. You will feel as though you've lost your precious child, and the loss will throw you into the Change Cycle. Now that you know how to deal with Square One, the loss will be easier; however, this section is here to prevent a total loss from happening in the first place. If you're already in an alien land, take a deep breath...help is on the way!

As I said in Chapter Two, it's vitally important to spend time with your children; however, it's not easy when they drive you crazy. It's difficult to maintain your own self-respect when faced with teens who are trying to become independent. They will question you at every turn, and your response will mark your mettle as a parent. As your kids age, you become less God-like in their eyes; your position becomes less automatically authoritative. Your sense of control with your older kids is tenuous in the best of times. I remember reading an interview with one of Hollywood's biggest stars who said that his kids were far from impressed by his big screen pedigree; to them he was just their dorky dad. This made me feel infinitely better, as my kids are continually looking at me like I'm crazy...come to think of it, my husband looks at me the same way! Fortunately, wacky seems to be a genetic predisposition that has served me quite well. My kids' friends love to come to our house, because it's fun: wacky is fun. Being wacky and laughing at life at its most trying is a powerful teaching tool as your kids become teenagers. In the worst of times, when pouty teenagers seemed to be all over my house, I knew that I was still connected to them if I could make them laugh...more often *at* me than *with* me, but as laughing is the object, I'm not picky.

If you have a good foundation of self–respect, a deeply held desire to aid your kids by using your values as a life raft, coupled with the ability to laugh at yourself and giggle at teen drama (I recommend laughing *with* them, not *at* them, as they are considerably less resilient than you are), then you have a good shot at keeping your teens close to you.

Use whatever feels authentic to you to make them laugh. For me, it's being incredibly wacky in a moment that doesn't call for it, like doing the M.C. Hammer dance in Walmart while shopping for hair supplies. This will have two effects: 1) it will make them giggle unexpectedly, like a kid, and 2) it will catch them off-guard, possibly embarrassing the snot out of them. It's good to shake their air of disdain from time to time. You can't take your teenagers too seriously; they're doing that all by themselves. The more you play into their drama, the bigger the drama will get. This is not a good thing for either one of you. If you remain lighthearted and silly, treating them like they are slightly addled, then they can realize that their behavior *is* silly sometimes. And maybe being silly is a preferred coping mechanism in the midst of all the drama her friends are tossing around.

I remember sitting across from my husband at a restaurant after my daily chat/text with my three college girls, and I got all teary eyed. The fact that my girls call or text me at least once a day to check in rates a big old +10 on my Body Compass. My fondest wish is for all parents to feel the deep sense of satisfaction my husband and I feel at how close we are to our teenagers. I know some parents who live in the same house with their teens, and they never talk; when our kids are home, we can't get away from them…and that's the way I like it.

My husband jokes that we have multiple bathrooms in our house, but the girls will usually use the one that's nearest us; hence, the reason my husband complains about having no personal space. With five females in the house, he has no one but the dog as a male companion, and he's neutered (the dog, not my husband). He has to lock himself in his bathroom to get a little peace and quiet; he complains, but, secretly, we both love it. We have a habit of watching television in our big king-sized bed, and we are rarely alone. More often than not, we will have two to four girls cuddling in bed with us. Every time this happens, I have the same sense of overwhelming gratitude that I experienced in that restaurant. As you have probably surmised by now, this situation was not always the norm; there were months that went by without seeing a smile on the face of my eldest or a conversation that was more than mono-syllabic with my middle child. By the time we got our bonus girl, I had changed my ways to include the tools in this book, and things were starting to turn around. Now, my teenagers and I adore each other (I've never had a real issue with my youngest; she's had a balanced mom since she started middle school) and, in the next few chapters, I'm going to show you how to open the lines of communication with your teens, so that you can have moments of overwhelming restaurant gratitude, as well.

The first step to disciplining during the teen years or repairing your existing relationship with your teen is the same. Take stock of where you are and practice acceptance...right here, right now. If your relationship is broken, accept it exactly as it is. The situation is here to teach you something. Use Byron Kate's Judge-Your-Neighbor worksheet[23] to write down all the ways your teenager is wrong, or lacking foresight, or just plain ticking you off. Then do the work on all those thoughts to see where in your life you are manifesting exactly the same traits and actions. When you do this detective work on yourself first, turning around all your own crappy thoughts, then, and only then, can you approach your teen. When you can forgive yourself for exhibiting the same traits

---

23 thework.com/thework-jyn.php

that your teen is driving you crazy with, then you can approach your teen with love. From a place of love, there's nothing you can't discuss. If you impose your rules from a place of "showing them who's in charge," that's ego…not love. If you discipline from a place of "doing the right thing, because that's our family value," that's love. From that place, anger isn't necessary. Disciplining without anger is tough, but it's necessary with teens. If you are holding a grudge against them from the start, they can feel it; you can't bridge that gap until you accept yourself and your teens. You don't have to love their actions, but you must show them that your love for them is never in question.

When you are disciplining your child, it is imperative to stay in your own business, cleaning up any thoughts you may have about why she got herself into the mess she's in. Punishing yourself for her behavior doesn't help anyone. Everybody makes mistakes, and your teens' mistakes are their business. Your business is to provide guidance (or punishment for bad choices) and support. This support includes not taking your kids' reactions personally. I'm not saying that they aren't punished for rude behavior, I'm just cautioning against disciplining from a place of righteous indignation…because that *never* works. If I had a nickel for every time I watched my teenagers stop listening at the first hint of my righteous indignation, I wouldn't need a day job. They stop listening after they hear that tone, or they put all their energy into distracting you so that things can go back to normal; either way, they aren't listening to your words.

Case in point, my middle child was having trouble in her senior year of high school. Her grades were slipping, largely due to the fact that she was skipping class enough for the school to call me.

My first reaction was about me, not her. "How dare she make me look bad! Here I am a parenting coach, and I can't even keep my kid in school…WTF! How can she be so irresponsible?" The outsized reaction to a relatively small issue (she still had all As and Bs, she was on target for a full in-state scholarship, and the skipping was handled before it affected her grades) was a clue that this was about me, not her. So I sat down and filled out a Judge-Your-Neighbor worksheet. I worked the thought, "Alyssa is not listening to me." After going through the questions, as I outlined in Chapter Five, I got to a turnaround thought that stopped me in my tracks, "I am not listening to Alyssa." This thought was as true as the original thought. Alyssa was having trouble, but all I did was preach at her about her grades. I was so concerned about her closing doors of opportunity with her behavior, that I didn't ask why she was doing it. I didn't accept the situation, so I couldn't learn the lesson it was trying to teach me. That lesson was to listen more than talk. Alyssa couldn't take responsibility for her grades with me hounding her any more than she could take responsibility for her weight struggle with me breathing down her neck. I needed to stop and listen to her.

When I did listen to her, it seemed that the class she was skipping most was taught by a teacher she loathed because of his arrogant attitude. Once she started skipping that class, it eroded her connection with her inner student. After listening to her, I still punished her. She was grounded for skipping class, but my righteous indignation was gone. When you discipline from a place of family values, the fight goes out of teenagers. They may not like the consequences, but they get it. And since I wasn't angry, she had nothing to rebel against. When I grounded her and took away her portals to her social life, she had nothing else to do besides study; that allowed her to re-discover her inner geek. It wasn't long before her actions provided a stronger lesson than my discipline ever could.

Even though she was now trying, she was distressed at how the teachers were less than supportive of her. I told her, "That's what happens when you skip class. Your behavior is disrespectful to your teacher, so why would they treat you any differently? Regardless of whether it's a good teacher or not, they still hold your GPA hostage while you're in their class. You're not getting back at a bad teacher by skipping class. You're just hurting yourself and your ability to have choices in which colleges will accept you. How about you respect yourself enough to show up: not just to class, but in your own life? I can't make you do that, baby; that must be your choice." She saw the consequences of being disrespectful to her teachers, and herself, by not showing up, and I saw how easily my righteous indignation could have derailed my parenting plan; we both learned a valuable lesson that has served us to this day. Today, Alyssa is on the dean's list at college and is bound and determined to go to graduate school.

Your own business is the only area where you can affect change; that's why staying in your own business is so important when you are disciplining teens. If you feel a sense of righteous indignation rising in your chest, and you're finding it a little hard to focus on thoughts of love toward your teen, stop and ask yourself, "Whose business am I in?" Refer back to Chapter Four for a refresher on Byron Katie's My Business/Your Business/God's Business tool. If you are in your own business and taking care of your own needs, your reaction to your teen's screw up will be much calmer. As a result, the punishment for said infraction will be much cleaner. If you can discipline your teen without anger, it will have a much more lasting effect. I use the line, "I'm not mad at you, honey, I'm just really disappointed in your choices," or "Acting like this is so out of character for you. What's going on?" Then I let her know that she will still be punished for poor choices, but I'm here to help figure out why she made the choice in the first place and what to do next time…if she wants my help. From this place, your teens can choose to talk to you or not; just realize that it's their choice, and their choice is not your business. Your business stops at devising and executing the punishment for a decision that went against your family values. Be very clear on why you're punishing your teen, and then explain it to them just as clearly.

In the above instance with Alyssa, she was punished for going against our family value of respecting others and ourselves enough to do the right thing. In this instance, the right thing was showing up to class. She was grounded for two weeks for skipping class; that meant no seeing her friends outside school and no leaving the house except to go to school. Since she is my social butterfly, this was a big punishment for her. With my other kids, I might take away cell phones or television. Social deprivation is the teen version of time-out in our house.

Again, use your Body Compass to devise a form of punishment that feels right to you. Whatever you choose, whether it's a deprivation-based punishment, like no phones or friends, or an active punishment, like washing windows or other ghastly chores, apply the punishment clearly and without emotion (other than by expressing disappointment in their choice that caused the punishment in the first place, if that feels right to you). When you discipline teenagers, remember they will really not like it and, by association, you, for a while. Whether or not they are mad at you is *their* business, not yours, so be prepared for the temperature in your house to drop twenty degrees. You just keep doing what you do and ignore the pouting. When my kids are grounded, I treat them exactly the same as normal. I joke with them and love them; the more normally I treat them (while maintaining their state of punishment), the quicker they will thaw. Remember, you are the one in charge; if your child balks at the punishment, then up the ante. If she is grounded for a week with no friend contact, and she breaks it, then the week turns into two weeks, or washing the windows turns into washing and vacuuming all the family vehicles. Your lack of emotion remains the same, regardless of where you are in the punishment cycle. That way, her bad behavior doesn't get a satisfying rise out of you; it only hurts her.

After the thaw, you can attempt to talk about whatever led to her bad choice. This is where the parenting rubber meets the road. If you can stay calm and resist the urge to preach, you can really make a connection with your teens. You can assure them that regardless of what they do, you will be there to love them and help them *when they ask*. This is the other side of discipline: offering your assistance with whatever plan they have devised to repair the damage that is a result of their bad choice. Then you wait for them to ask for your help. Teaching your kids to ask for help is an excellent way to ensure that they will get their needs met after they leave the protection of your presence. If you don't teach them to ask for help by asking *you* for help, you are shorting them a very important life skill. If you have a problem asking for help, it's going to be very difficult to teach it to your teenager.

If you're a control freak, like me, you've probably developed an "I have to do it all by myself to do it right" story. Just know that this is your own invention. We all need help, and the sooner you admit it, the happier your life will be. It took cancer for me to admit that perhaps I couldn't do everything all by myself; at least I couldn't do everything and stay healthy. As I've said before, we must do our own work before we even think of asking our children to do their work. To this end, look at your to-do list with a jaundiced eye. If you have tasks on your list that send your Body Compass into negative territory, use the Martha Beck tool called *The 3 Bs* on them: Bag it, Barter it, or Better it. If you don't have to do that thing today, or at all really, Bag it; it has no business on your list, so put it on the Universe's list (this is from my Girl Power Transformer worksheet, which has a list with your to-do items and a much longer list of items for the Universe to handle. If your item isn't on your list, then it's on the Universe's list. Just taking it off your list can give you some breathing space and energy to do the things that *are* on your list). If you can't Bag it, like, for instance, laundry, perhaps you can Barter it. Ask your spouse, friend, or mom to do your laundry, and you will do something on their list that they hate; yes this will require you to ask for help from another person (isn't this where we started this whole line of thought?). The third way is the easiest: Better it. Find something that you love to do (use your Five Things list from Chapter One) and then do that *while* you're doing the laundry…play music, burn incense, dance or, better yet, do all three at once. I don't do laundry anymore without my iPod blaring Motown. My kids just LOVE this!

When you can ask for help with something as innocuous as your to-do list, then you can expand that into asking for help in other areas. I've gotten especially good at asking for help from my teens with small tasks here and there, without an expectation that they will comply. It's amazing how releasing the expectation leads to them helping me much more than when I was all stressed out by thinking that I had to do everything myself. Back then I would petulantly demand that they help me because (cue violins), "It isn't fair that I have to do everything around here." This display would often finish with the grand finale foot stomp and door slam…that would be my foot and my door. Since I didn't really expect them to help me, I would end up doing it myself, thereby proving my petulant thought true. Why would anyone want to help in that situation? Now, I don't have to even ask my girls to clear the table or do the dishes; they do it because they love me, and they know it really helps me. Now that I am better at asking for help, my teens follow my example. This leads me to my next teen parenting tip… lead by example.

CHAPTER FIFTEEN

Leading by Example

I've said before how ineffective the "Do as I say, not as I do" philosophy is with teenagers; actually that philosophy doesn't really work with anyone. If you think it does, reflect upon times when you were in a situation where a person in a position of power over you subscribed to that policy; how did that feel to you? I can work myself into a lather about people who preach piety on Sunday after posting dubious pictures on Facebook from Saturday night. The lather then returns me right back to my own life and to where *I'm* being hypocritical; then, I proceed to clean that nastiness up! Leading by example is the best form of guidance you can give your teen. We have used all the coaching tools up to this point to determine what our path in life is, and we have begun to use baby steps to toddle down the path toward that life. Applying these tools on a daily basis is crucial in showing your teens the most efficient way to make their dreams a reality.

This reminds me of an incident with my youngest when my knee-jerk guilt for leaving my kids almost blew a beautiful Monday morning paddle boarding session. I had purchased a new car the previous Saturday, and Emily was thrilled with all its bells and whistles (a Honda Pilot that I absolutely love!). As I was putting the finishing touches on her lunch (peanut butter and jelly, check, snacks, check, appropriately hilarious notes, check), I saw a pod of dolphins surface just at the end of our dock. I squealed and screamed upstairs, "DOLPHINS!!! Emmy, Mommy is going to go paddle boarding right now; can Daddy take you to school?"

Her sad face appeared above the banister, and she said, "Aw, Mommy, I really wanted you to take me!"

The aforementioned guilt started talking to me, "Your child needs you, and you're going to go play with dolphins? What kind of a mother are you?" I almost acquiesced without thinking, but then the "lead by example" concept popped into my head. Paddle boarding with dolphins is a spiritual experience for me. Every time I do it, I feel expansive; it helps my writing, and I'm a kinder, more generous person because of that spiritual awakening. So I asked, "Emmy, it's really important to Mommy to go spend time in nature. Are you sure Daddy can't take you to school?"

She replied, "Can he drive me in your new car?"

Aha! It was the car she wanted; she didn't care who drove it. If I hadn't stood up for my own needs, I wouldn't have inquired further; I would have driven her to school, missed the dolphins, and felt cheated for the rest of the day. This is a relatively unimportant scene in the grand scheme of parenting four kids, but it meant a lot to me. I stood up for my own needs; I gave my daughter a chance to be generous, and I patterned for her what it looks like to follow your heart. So I guess it wasn't so small after all!

Standing up for your "me" time is not the only way to pattern healthy choices for your kids. Teaching time management is crucial to avoid burnout in high school and, to a lesser extent, middle school (I talk more about this in Chapter 17). Again, before you can teach time management, you need to have a handle on it yourself. I have a very good friend who I call the Time Goddess. Her name is Jill Farmer, and she wrote a whole book devoted to this subject called *There's Not Enough Time and Other Lies We Tell Ourselves*[24]. I highly recommend this book for anyone who feels like they have too much to do and too little time to do it… that would be everyone I know. The parts of Jill's message that I like the most are her division of tasks into those that you choose to do today, and then everything else. She suggests that you pull three to five crucial items off your "to-do sometime" list and add them onto your "to-do today" list. You can then peel off little two-minute tasks in ten-minute blocks of time. This is similar to the way I've composed my Girl Power Transformer worksheet; in fact, I've added Jill's two-minute tasks to my worksheet. Once you start using your to-do list as a tool to streamline your day, instead of a club to beat yourself up with because you're not doing enough, then you can begin to lead your life with intention. Jill writes "Things I get to do" at the top of her list, because it really is our choice how we spend our time. We might as well appreciate the fact that we are healthy enough to have a to-do list at all!

The next Lead-by-Example idea is to become self-centered. You wouldn't think that it's important to encourage your teen to be self-centered, but that's exactly what I'm recommending. However, this is a different kind of self-centered. If you think of your heart as being the center of your body, then being self-centered is the same as heart-centered. You want your teens to make decisions

---

24 www.amazon.com/Theres-Enough-Time-Ourselves-ebook/dp/B00AQ41K40/ref
=sr_1_1?ie=UTF8&qid=1379781147&sr=8-1&keywords=there%27s+not+enough
+time

based upon their own inner compass and their Inner Guide, not what's going on around them. It doesn't matter if they are in a big-city high school or a rural schoolhouse; because of the Internet, our kids are all exposed to the same stuff. For girls, it's the mean-girl syndrome, when girls cut down other girls because they are competing for a boy's affection, or a skewed self-image based upon the degrading media images of "unless you're sexy, you don't count"; and for boys, it's the "I'm too cool to be kind" and "Don't show weakness" attitudes, especially toward girls or smaller boys. This crap is viral; I see it everywhere I travel.

Brene Brown speaks eloquently of how shame plays into these attitudes in her book *Daring Greatly*, a must read for parents…and any other human being who wants to lead a more wholehearted life. Brown talks about ways to develop shame resilience that have transformed my parenting. If you are living in shame, you cannot help your child with their problems. Her shame resilience is based upon empathy and connection; both are integral to Plugged-In Parenting. If you're practicing self-care and filling yourself up, you are less likely to jump to the conclusion that you are not enough; a sense of lack creates a block to empathy. When we focus on how much we suck, it is impossible to be truly connected and empathetic; we are too wrapped up in supporting the case for how lacking we are. And if we are so awful, why would anyone want to connect with us? Shame and lack-based thinking are isolating; we exclude ourselves from the people who could help support us.

The best antidote to exclusion-based thinking is to teach your teens to be heart-centered and, yes, the only way to teach your teens is by practicing this yourself. Buddhists have a concept of "right speech" and "right action" that sums up my version of being heart-centered.[25] Right speech means, "to tell the truth, to speak friendly, warm, and gently, and to talk only when necessary" and right action means, "to act kindly and compassionately, to be honest, to respect the belongings of others, and to keep sexual relationships harmless to others." These concepts seem pretty basic, but if you walk the halls of most high schools, and some middle schools, these basic ideals are difficult to find. So if you want to teach the importance of Right Speech and Right Action, open a dialogue with your teen. Ask him if he's ever heard of these Buddhist principles; tell him you've been reading about them, and you want his opinion. You don't have to be a Buddhist to appreciate these concepts, just like you don't have to be a Christian to appreciate the beauty of Christ's teachings, especially as they relate to treating others as you wish to be treated. By asking his opinion, you will draw your teen in. Teens love to opine on their world…all you have to do is ask (without an agenda to "teach them a lesson").

Then, of course, the next step is to practice Right Speech and Right Action in your own life. If you've introduced the concept, and then practiced it on your own, you have a reference point for a follow-up conversation with your teen about how it's going for both of you practicing these concepts. You can talk about how difficult it is to rise above the drama, how little things can make a big difference, and how clueless or plugged in other boys or girls are. The important thing here is that you are talking *with* your teen, not *at* them.

If you are distanced from your teen, starting a dialogue about a new subject opens the door a little bit. It may not work

---

25 www.thebigview.com/buddhism/eightfoldpath.html

the first time, and that's okay. Just keep at it, always dropping the expectation that it will fix everything. If you put that kind of pressure on one conversation, it will end up being your only conversation. If you can look at it like it's a tiny baby step on the path back to a relationship, then your expectations will be low. I frequently tell my clients, and myself, that the closer you can keep your expectations to reality, the less often frustration will raise its head. Expectations are different than goals; goals are where you are headed based upon your Inner Guide compass, and expectations are the Inner Judge chatter you have about that goal. When the inner chatter is supportive, it can be crucial to actually reaching said goal. However, when the Inner Judge is peeing in your cornflakes, it would be helpful to look at the expectation behind the chatter.

I have a running conversation (usually in my head, but sometimes aloud *mostly* when I'm alone) where I forgive myself for slip ups, saying things like, "That's okay, sweetie. We'll get it next time." This is much more helpful that the chatter I used to have, "WTF! What are you doing? That was so stupid!" I used to talk to myself in a way I would never speak to anyone else; in fact, if someone spoke to my kids the way I used to talk to myself, I would have whupped 'em, Mama-Bear style. If this describes the way you talk to yourself, it would behoove you to practice a little Right Speech with yourself. The nicer you are to yourself, the more your children will recognize that as normal. Then when someone doesn't treat them that way, they will see it as a sign to walk away.

The first step in practicing Right Speech and Right Action as it pertains to your own sweet self is to recognize your own gifts.

I call this having a JP moment. My great-grandfather's name was James Plew, and he was a bigger-than-life character who went from orphan to millionaire by virtue of an adventurous spirit and an inventive mind. He actually *was* an inventor. Among his inventions were the triangular bicycle seat with the springs under the back (it was originally called the Plew saddle) and the nasal inhaler that was later purchased by Vicks. I believe I am connected to him in my puzzle cracking ability. I can look at a hairy situation, and a solution to streamline it will float into my mind. I invented that solution. I also come up with inventions to make things easier or more efficient all the time. I haven't brought any of them into production yet, but maybe when all of my kids are off on their own, my inventive mind will take me there. Every time I acknowledge my JP moments, I feel a little bit more solid and authentic.

Find things that come easily to you and write them down. Now acknowledge that these things are valuable. Too often, if something comes easily to us, we dismiss it as something everyone knows or does. That is not true. Your special gifts are God-given to you; acknowledge them as such, and quit beating yourself up about the stuff that doesn't come as easily. Beating yourself up never motivates you to do better; it just makes you feel crummy and ineffective, which is not a good starting place for your best work. When you can recognize what you do well and begin practicing Right Speech and Right Action with yourself, *then* you can approach your teen about doing the same thing. One way to enforce this is to point out all the things about your teen that you appreciate, and point them out often. Whether you do it in a note that is tucked into their lunch or book bag or aloud to their face, use your Right Speech and Right Action to tell and show your teens exactly how amazing they are on a daily basis. It will start a pattern of confidence that they can carry with them throughout their day.

In my career as a parent, I've tried many different ways to develop my children into the type of person I would want to help as an employer or as a mentor. When you and your kids practice Right Speech and Right Action and value your own gifts, using baby steps to bring that practice into your everyday lives, you will slowly develop a balanced and positive outlook. Other people, employers and teachers, can feel that balanced self-respect, and it makes them want to help your teen. Think of all the kids they deal with who aren't respectful or balanced. If you practice the things in this chapter, you will turn out a kid who's a pleasure to teach or employ. As a result of this balance, I've seen my kids succeed in the same situation where others do not.

Another corollary to treating other people with respect is to suck up to those in a position of power, when necessary. I learned this concept when I was interviewing a candidate for a job. I was on the board of a non-profit agency, and this gentleman was interviewing for the agency director's position. When we asked him about his most effective qualification, he immediately said, "I'm great at sucking up to the right people in order to get things done." I laughed at the time, but I realized how true his words really were. This is related to my habit of taking responsibility for whatever went wrong, just to move past the finger pointing to a solution. When your kid is faced with a dictatorial (a.k.a. insecure, pompous windbag) teacher who may be threatened by his talent, sucking up is the way to go. It doesn't matter if the teacher is wrong and your kid is right; you fighting his battles will not teach him how to survive a similar person as a future employer or coworker. If you can teach your kids the power of sucking up and swallowing their pride, they will be light years ahead; as I've said before, that sucky teacher still holds their GPA hostage.

My middle child had a teacher who was giving her a hard time in one of her college classes. Alyssa thought she was flaky and incompetent, and the teacher didn't think much of Alyssa either. I asked her if she'd been sucking up (this is always the first question I ask when my kids come home with a bad teacher story). She said that she hadn't. I suggested she try it, since she couldn't get out of the class. The next time we talked about the class was a month and a half later, when Alyssa informed me that she had turned her grade around to an A+. Not only had she sucked up by asking questions in class and volunteering for tasks, but she had also developed compassion for the teacher, seeing a different side of her once she saw Alyssa as a friend instead of a foe.. Sucking up is really just an intention-based connection. When normally you would walk away, but you can't because the difficult person is in a position of power over you, then try sucking up. It can't hurt, and you might just find that once you stop trying to change the other person, you can begin to find areas in common. The connection that started in a contrived sucking-up place may end in a place of mutual respect.

People tend to look at me and my kids and think we are lucky… and we are. However, luck can be crafted. The more connections I make by being respectful of other people, or sucking up when the situation calls for it, the more people want to help me. Making your own luck starts with respecting your own gifts and talents. Once you have established, or re-established, a dialogue with your teen by leading by example, and both of you are operating from a level playing field of Right Speech and Right Action, then you can search for ways to improve the chances for your teen to be successful socially and academically. This involves shrinking the big hairy high school down into a smaller group. Next up: preparing our teens for the real world.

CHAPTER SIXTEEN

Team Sports: The Good, the Bad, and the Ugly

Life in the real world is tough; it's especially tough if you think that you have to do it all alone. I love team sports, because they teach kids how to work together. Working within a team is a valued skill in the corporate environment, and it also puts a different twist on what success means to girls…this is *good*. I have a fourteen-year-old who is deeply in love with volleyball. She is the first kid of mine who has been involved with team sports, and I think it just might be the antidote to the aforementioned sucky freshman year. I have taken note of the difference in attitude of the teen girls who play sports versus the girls who don't. The sporty types are much more interested in cool stuff like being strong and fast than uncool stuff like being arm candy for some cocky boy. I know there are boys out there who aren't solely interested in slaking their raging hormonal thirst with a pretty girl, but I don't need to warn my girls about *them*. When my kid's coach heard one of the players referring to one of her teammates as a "girl," the coach said, "We are not just girls, we are girl *athletes*." She then pointed out that, as a girl athlete, they are held to a higher standard; they have to be strong *and* smart. I almost cried with relief when I heard this.

There's so much crappy media out there telling girls that to get ahead they need to be sexy, so that they can get a man. As if that's a goal to make them more complete. This puts my teeth on edge. Not only is the image false, but it sets up a situation where boys and girls are pitted against each other; or worse, girls are pitted against other girls as competition for a boy's attention. I believe the antidote to this is shifting attention away from looks and toward goals. Team sports shrink the whole Universe of girls down to a small group who are all pulling together for a common goal…pun fully intended. This banding together is the opposite of what you often find in high school…the Mean-Girl Syndrome.

The Mean-Girl Syndrome is at the heart of the movie *Mean Girls* and the book that inspired it by Rosalind Wiseman[26]. This is one of my favorite movies, because it discusses a serious issue with humor… my favorite method of instruction. I told one of my teen clients the other day that my vision is a world where the Mean-Girl Syndrome is only discussed in sociology class as an aberration in history, like slavery. The idea that "popular" girls are expected to be nasty to "unpopular" girls is a situation whose time has passed, and it's my mission to teach girls that they have a choice in how they treat their sisters. I want to show them how important the support of other girls is to their future success.

After a trip to Africa, I rebranded my company to reflect the way the lionesses run their pride. The lionesses are in charge of the pride, but the group is only as strong as the support given to and from each individual (spoiler alert: this is the topic of my next

---

26 *Queen Bees and Wannabes*, by Rosalind Wiseman

book!). As I watched the pride work to hunt and care for their young, I thought that the strong bonds of kinship are exactly what's missing in female relationships today. Girls are turning against each other, starting in middle school, often using the affection of a boy as an excuse to attack another girl. This situation comes up with every one of my teen clients. The only way to solve this issue is to talk about it. Talk to your teenage girl about it like it's important because, to her, it's crucial. Stress the fact that the "mean girls" have their own insecurities they are covering up with bitchy behavior, and sometimes the only way to handle their bitchiness is to ignore it. Your teen isn't going to change the situation alone, but if she is taking very good care of herself (see self-care tips in the next chapter) and surrounding herself with other kids who have similar goals and dreams, then the nasty chatter doesn't hurt so much. It becomes like a two-year-old throwing a tantrum; it's annoying, but it doesn't have anything to do with you. The Mean-Girl Syndrome is much less apparent on the court or the playing field because, unless she's really a superstar, the less "popular" players don't give a fig about what the mean girl says.

The Mean-Girl Syndrome is a symptom of a larger problem that can also be solved with a team mentality. As we all know, our kids are subjected to increasing levels of electronic media, and the recent numbers are significantly higher than the last five-year study: "Today, 8–18-year-olds devote an average of 7 hours and 38 minutes (7:38) to using entertainment media across a typical day (more than 53 hours a week). And because they spend so much of that time "media multitasking" (using more than one medium at a time), they actually manage to pack a total of 10 hours and 45 minutes (10:45) worth of media content into those

7½ hours. The amount of time spent with media increased by an hour and seventeen minutes a day over the past five years, from 6:21 in 2004 to 7:38 today. And because of media multitasking, the total amount of media content consumed during that period has increased from 8:33 in 2004 to 10:45 today."[27]These statistics shocked me, but just look at any teen; his face is plastered to his phone or computer most of the time.

With all this time spent in front of a screen, our kids are being subjected to the media's version of how boys and girls should relate…and it's not healthy. My middle child did her senior project on body image, and she spoke about how you look is *not* the sum of who you are. In the course of her research, she found a great website, www.missrepresentation.org, that is trying to change the way the media portrays women. They believe, and I agree with them, that until we take a stand and refuse to buy products from companies who use ad campaigns that demean women, the media will not change.

In order to counteract the media's less-than-respectful treatment of girls, we need to change the messages our girls are receiving at home. As parents, we must tell our girls that if they don't respect each other, why would the boys act any better? If we want our daughters to treat each other with respect, we must teach them that girls are all on the same team, or in lioness-speak they are all part of the same Pride. Each and every girl can embody the lioness power I witnessed in Africa, because girl power is only as strong as the respect and support of their Pride. When girls have the support of their Pride, their self-respect quotient rises, and this results in an increase in their own inner pride as well. I believe

---

27 Kaiser Family Foundation www.kff.org/entmedia/entmedia012010nr.cfm

that putting our girls on teams is step one in fostering mutual respect, instead of the divisive treatment that exists off the court. Encouraging your kids to join a team—any team, it doesn't have to be sports (band, forensics, civics organization, or the chess club will do just fine)—shrinks the whole high school down to a more manageable size, thereby giving your child a fighting chance of having a group of friends who support her…this is also *good*. With the power of the Pride behind us, we can accomplish anything. This goes for moms as well.

In my youth, I always thought that once I had the right man, I wouldn't need a lot of friends (just like my momma told me), hence, the multiple marriages. That's too heavy a burden for one relationship to bear, and my previous two buckled under the strain. It was only when I married the party guy that I realized the importance of friendships. My husband has a Pride of close friends who have been together for over thirty years; that's a powerful dynamic to watch. The beauty of a healthy Pride is that different members serve different roles. This is an idea that has been expanded by Shasta Nelson in her book *Friendships Don't Just Happen*[28]. Shasta's book has completely changed the way I look at friendship. If we are feeling lonely, it's not that we are less valuable; it's just that we have some friendship circles that are a little sparse. Once we acknowledge that all friendships are not supposed to Best Friends Forever (BFF), then we can move forward to fill our other circles with Pride members who belong there. It takes pressure off existing friendships to be something they're not.

In Shasta's continuum, five circles of friendship are separated by time spent together as well as level of intimacy. This was

28 www.amazon.com/Friendships-Dont-Just-Happen-GirlFriends/

important for me to learn. Just because I click with someone, and we have the same values, doesn't mean they make it into my inner circle, unless we also have frequency built into the friendship... and that's okay. This is something we can teach our kids: different kinds of friendships serve different purposes. If they think that all friendships have to be a BFF, then they will put so much pressure on a less intimate friendship, that it will likely blow up. If they can realize, however, that different levels of closeness exist within the Pride, then they can build each circle to a level where they feel supported and balanced.

Now we will look at the not-so-positive aspects of teams, specifically: going overboard on the number of hours spent on extracurricular activities to the point that your child is exhausted is *bad*. I talked about this in Chapter Two, and I will go more in depth in the next chapter, but suffice it to say that when your child's extracurricular activities eat into family time, it can turn a great thing into something harmful. Be aware that just because the next-door neighbors' kids are playing four sports and burning more time, money, and gas than an NFL team, does not mean you have to do the same thing. It's a different version of keeping up with the Joneses that can be just as harmful to your family life. To prevent this, the rule in our house is "one thing at a time"; pick one extracurricular activity at a time. With the amount of homework assigned in my daughter's honors classes, there is no way she can play more than one sport and, a) still finish all her homework, b) have downtime to clown around with her friends, and c) get enough sleep. Adjust your child's schedule in a way that feels right to you, not what is popular or what the coach says is okay. You are the parent and, as such, you are in charge of how much time your child spends away from home.

When too much time is spent away from home, kids can forget what a comforting structure feels like. If your family is rushing around trying to fill every possible moment with extra-curricular activities, something has to give. As we all know how important school time is, it's usually downtime and family time that suffers. Since your child replenishes their sense of family values and belonging during family time, when it is scrapped for activity time, your kid will feel stressed. Stressed out kids will beget stressed out parents. When we are stressed, we start trying to regain control, and that usually means upping the discipline...to make us feel more in charge. Then we start disciplining not from a place of family values, but from a place of need: a need for control, a need for stability, and a need to be right. As a parent, this need to be right is not healthy and, taken to extremes, can set a bad example for your kid...especially on the playing field. This leads me to my next topic...the ugly team parent.

If you have been to a children's sporting event in the last ten years, you have probably witnessed the Ugly Parent. It's kind of like the Stage Mom, only sweatier. These parents are so invested in their children's "success" that they lose sight of the important lessons that competition teaches. What happened to parents setting an example for their children to learn good sportsmanship? I see parents who are on the sidelines *screaming* at their children, the coaches, and the referees; this is *ugly*. I understand wanting your child to succeed; we all want that. However, if winning is more important than playing a good game, you are short-circuiting the beauty of team sports. You are teaching your child that it's okay to bully other people just to get your own way. That is not a recipe for success in the real world. These parents are setting their child up for disappointment when they become an adult who has to play well with others in order to hold down a job.

You cannot solve your lack of a sporting career by living vicariously through your child; all you can do is support them in whatever activity lights them up inside. If you want to play sports, join an adult team; don't satisfy your need for validation with micro-managing your child's play. It will not fulfill your needs, and it certainly won't make your kid want to be part of a team. Teams are good for your kids, for all the reasons we have listed in this chapter; don't blow it for them! If you recognize yourself or someone you know in the Ugly Parent description, don't worry... there is hope! Take all the energy you've been pouring into making your kid a success on the field and put it into finding your own Pride. If the Ugly Parents had a circle of friends to fill them up, they might not be quite as interested in micro-managing their child's sports activities. It's amazing how healthy circles of friends will change your outlook on what is really important.

Team sports prepare our kids for life in the real world, and isn't that our number-one mission as parents? Like anything, however, there are downsides. I believe the upside potential of shrinking the school to a manageable size and the intrinsic power that exists in groups of individuals pulling for the same goal is worth it. If your child picks a team, any team, of like-minded people, they will start building their own Pride. They will go further and have more fun on the journey if they are surrounded by support. As soon as we accept the possible downside of team sports, then we can start to craft our family schedule to include team bonding without the all-encompassing time suck that more than one sport or club at a time can entail. Speaking of time, let's talk about how our teens need time and energy management as much, if not more, than we do.

CHAPTER SEVENTEEN

Self-Care for Teens:
Energy and Time Management

Self-care is important for teens, but no one is telling them that. They are so concerned with fitting in that they can lose track of who they are inside. High school is a fun-fest for their Inner Judge, who is always comparing their actions and thoughts to those of the successful or "popular" kids; these two definitions don't always go together. Some popular kids *are* successful, but other popular kids are well known just because they manifest a circus of drama, where they hold the ringleader position. The problem is that your kid's Inner Judge doesn't know the difference; she is looking to fit in at any cost. When the Inner Judge is running the show, the voice of the Inner Guide is muzzled. Creative play is shunned for a more outward focus on social convention, and a good night's sleep is bartered for a minute-to-minute social connection. Without creative time and sufficient sleep, you won't need to worry about time management, because your kid will be living in overwhelm… and that's the worst neighborhood in town. Teenagers are just bigger, smellier kids; they are also young adults. It's this dichotomy that makes high school so challenging. How do they become young adults without leaving behind the wonder and beauty of childhood? Creative play…that's how!

I have a client who is a pediatrician. She has a theory that when we create something with our hands, we feel better. Her dream is to have a facility that uses creative crafts to treat loneliness and depression in teens. I think it's a brilliant idea! I have seen the efficacy of her theory in my own life and in the lives of my kids. When my eldest was going through tough times, I could expect to see her slapping paint on canvas when I opened her door. Once she created a brilliant painting that is vibrantly red and orange; she did it when she was *really* mad at me for grounding her. It fairly screams indignant rage, but she kept it on the canvas…and she felt better afterwards. I use creativity as a break between writing sprints, because I make my living with my ability to put words on paper in a way that conveys what's important to me. If I'm disconnected from my creativity, my writing suffers; if I'm stuck, I can pick up knitting needles and the feel of the yarn through my fingers will ground me in a way nothing else can. My doctor client started me knitting, and now it has balanced my life in a way I never anticipated.

If your teen doesn't have a creative outlet already, maybe you can find one together. Take a painting class or a knitting class with your teen; then you can both use the crafting to balance out the pressures in your life. Drama has no hold on creativity; as soon as you start to create something with your hands, you begin to realize that all the worries you left behind are just lack and fear stories that your Inner Judge is spinning to keep you "safe." You can choose to listen, or back away and do something creative; take the energy you were putting into your thoughts and put it into your hands instead. And then teach your kid to do the same thing.

I've noticed that my youngest will put more time into any class project if it involves art. In history class, she created a foldout bulletin as a way to demonstrate her knowledge of American History. It wasn't an art class, but she used her art to make it more fun. And because she approached the project with creativity, she got an A. Teachers love creative kids; it makes their job more interesting. Isn't it nice that it makes the task more fun for the student as well? I've told my little one that she needs to remember how much better studying is when she builds art into it. This will be important for her into college; when she feels stuck, she needs to start creating something to move past the block. All of this presupposes that your child isn't exhausted from too little sleep.

How much sleep your teen needs is a rarely discussed issue in high school. When I talk to high school students, this is one of the most hotly debated topics. No one argues that proper sleep is necessary for growth, both physical and mental, and lack of sleep can lead to a host of problems. My kids have always been big sleepers, because I set up an environment where that was the norm; see me following my own advice and leading by example! I used to have a big problem with insomnia until I read an article that gave some hints to cure it; I followed their instructions, and it worked. The program that I followed was comprised of a few behavioral guidelines; these suggestions work just as well for teens as they do for parents. If you or your teen is having trouble falling, or staying, asleep, try these simple steps:

1. Start with the time you want to wake up, then back up 7.5 to 8 hours; that's the time you need to be asleep. I can already hear you kvetching, "I don't have enough time to sleep 7.5 to 8 hours," to which I reply, "You must *make*

it happen, if not for you, for your children." Your kids deserve a parent who is well rested enough to be patient and plugged-in. I'm convinced that one of the reasons I had debilitating migraines, carried extra weight, and ultimately got cancer was chronic sleep deprivation. *Take the time to sleep.*

2. Now that you have a "go-to-sleep" time, back up another hour; from this time on, you will not stare at any backlit screens. No television, computer, iPad, iPhone, or gaming device…nothing with a back-lit screen. You can still use a Kindle, because it's not backlit. Or perhaps you can just read a real paper book; I'm sure there's a passel of publishers who really wish you would!

3. Establish a bedtime routine; I choose reading something not too exciting. The article recommended a hot bath or shower and warm milk, but neither of these appeal to me.

4. Make your bedroom dark and cool with no clocks you can see from your bed. Since I'm menopausal, my bedroom is like a dark meat locker: 65 degrees in winter, 70 in the summer. Some people like white noise; I like quiet, so I sleep with earplugs. Granted, if you're a single mom or dad, earplugs are not the way to go. I'm fortunate to have my hubby who has no problem sleeping or waking up when there's a screaming child to tend…or waking me up to tend said child. When you wake up, reverse the dark, cold room; warm up and turn on bright lights. This will tell your brain that sleepy time is finished.

5. Now that you've established your routine, don't vary from it. That means going to bed and arising at roughly the

same time seven nights a week, at least until you reset your body clock…then you can add in some later nights, but try not to vary more than a few hours. If you are suffering from insomnia, I wouldn't vary at all for a few months.

Sleep is crucial for your health and the health of your teen, especially teen athletes. When it comes to your teen's sleep habits, their body clock is often working against them in high school. Adolescents have a natural tendency to fall asleep later in their teen years; an average time is eleven p.m., because, during adolescence, their melatonin production starts later at night than when they were in elementary school. With most high schools starting early, this leaves our teens with sleep deprivation, which can lead to lower test scores, poor athletic performance, and a higher incidence of depression, not to mention driving in a less-than-alert state. According to Nemours.org, a fabulous resource for information on teen health, "More than half of teens surveyed reported that they have driven a car drowsy over the past year and 15 percent of students in the 10th to 12th grades drive drowsy at least once a week. The National Highway Safety Traffic Administration estimates that more than 100,000 accidents, 40,000 injuries, and 1,500 people are killed in the U.S. every year in crashes caused by drivers who are simply tired. Young people under the age of 25 are far more likely to be involved in drowsy driving crashes."[29]

This website suggests that an appropriate amount of sleep for a teen is 8.5 to 9.5 hours per night. Share the above sleep routine

---

29 This is from an excellent article by Nemours.org that can be found at kidshealth. org/teen/your_body/take_care/how_much_sleep.html#. I encourage you and your teen to read the article, as it's full of great information.

with your teens, using those numbers as optimal. Bribe them to try the routine for a week or two; the results will keep them on it. They will have a better attitude, less overwhelm, better resilience to nasty bugs, both bacterial and social, and, as their mind clears, their grades will improve. Again, I implore you to try the sleep routine first to see the results. Then you can tell your teen about your experience, and then *let it go*! They will come to you if they want more information, *if* you release the expectation that they need to come and talk to you. When they see positive results of your new routine, they will eventually ask you about it. It may not happen quickly but, then again, that's not your business. Be patient and release the outcome. A focus on getting enough sleep will help them not only in high school, but also in college and beyond. If their routine involves adequate sleep, then they will be fresher and less stressed in their post college job, as well.

I named my first company A Life in Balance, LLC, because finding balance is my life's work. I spent the majority of my life being *way* out of balance: I was bulimic in high school (classic teen girl imbalance); then I studied myself sick to attain a level of academic perfection that would land me in an Ivy League school, only to sabotage my application process; then I took that perfectionism into my parenting and my job, and turned out a product that was less than healthy in both areas. Now, however, I have seen the error of my ways…I have learned to say, "No."

An important life lesson to teach your kids is how to achieve balance, and the first step in achieving balance is to learn to choose what you want to do and what you *don't* want to do. When it comes to school/extracurricular balance, saying "no" is an extremely important skill. I believe the ability to say "no" is a saving grace in high school, not only socially but academically, as well. And, of course, you need to learn how to say "no" before you can teach it to your child. This is not a valued skill in our work harder, play harder to get ahead society.

My friend Jill Farmer[30], whose book I mentioned earlier, told me about how she says "no," and it resonated with me so much that I've incorporated it into my everyday decision making. After I tried it, I talked with my teens about it, and they have told me that it's been very helpful for them as well. The way I apply her method is as follows: when I'm faced with someone asking me to do something for them or their organization, I use Jill's formula. I ask myself three questions:

1. Do I want to do it?
2. Does it support my values/passion/vision?
3. Does it fit in the available time I have right now?

If the answer to two of these questions is "no," then my answer is "no." This works with social and work-related obligations. When you start asking yourself these questions about tasks on your to-do list, it will aid you in finding more time. In the hectic world of high school, finding more time for your teen will make you his hero. However, don't take that hero worship too seriously, or it will feed that ego place that we have spent many pages slimming down. Teach your teen time management and how to say "no," because it's the right thing to do, not because you want to be right.

I mentioned lists for teens back in Chapter Fifteen, and now I'm going to show you how to help your teens help themselves. The method of time management I like the best for teens is to write everything that's swimming around in their head down

---

on paper. I remember when one of my high school seniors was stressing out about all the homework she had, but she wouldn't write it down. I said, "Write it down, and we'll tackle it one by one." She didn't want to write it down, because she thought it would be too overwhelming to see it on paper (this is not the first time I've heard this, so I know that other teens think the same thing). That is faulty logic. The tasks remain the same whether they are in your head or on paper. However, when you write them down, you don't have to remember them; they are right there in black and white. Then you can put all the energy you were using trying to remember the tasks into actually doing them. Furthermore, when you complete a task, you get to cross it off your list; something that I like better than chocolate and margaritas put together!

Once your teen has all their tasks written down, if she feels overwhelmed, then she's taking too big a bite. Overwhelm is not an invitation to white knuckle your way through something, it's a sign to back up and break your list into smaller lists. This is where you want to introduce the baby step concept to your teen. Remember, a baby step is a step so small that you would characterize it as "ridiculously easy." I always think about Zoolander saying "ridiculously good looking." When I am explaining this to clients, I often use the Zoolander accent to say "ridiculously easy."[31] This may be one reason people look at me strangely and shake their heads, but I'm getting used to it. The more you can pattern the beauty of baby steps by using them in your own life, the more comfortable your teens will be in trying them. They won't tell you they're doing it, because that may make you right; but you may

---

31 Zoolander is a 2001 Ben Stiller comedy that we have watched more times than I'd care to admit.

find lists lying around the house as their stress levels ease. If this happens, I highly recommend *not* saying, "Oh good, you're using the baby steps. I told you they would work!" That will make it your idea, and they will drop it like a hot potato. Just bask in the fact that it *was* your idea, and it worked.

The more you can fill yourself up with proper rest, manage your time, and learn how to say "no" to people and events that don't line up with your value system, the more your teen will learn the same lessons by following your example. We've spent many pages together learning how to set up a home support system that will help you and your children succeed in your pursuit of a joyful life. So what happens when it all goes wrong, and they bring home a friend/boyfriend/girlfriend that doesn't blend with your family values? Cue scary music...enter the Emotional Vampire.

CHAPTER EIGHTEEN

Protecting Your Teens from Emotional Vampires

I taught a class on conflict resolution not too long ago, and I entitled it "How to Survive and Thrive When You're Surrounded by Emotional Vampires." It was a class for adults, but this is a hugely important topic for teens as well. It reminds me of a time when my middle daughter, Alyssa, was hanging out with a boy who won first prize in the broken wing contest. This daughter specializes in broken wing repair; unfortunately, she didn't stop with animals. She used to make it her mission to be the home for broken boyfriends as well. It's never a good thing when you set eyes upon your daughter's beloved and think "OMG, WTF!" and a host of other acronyms that stand for words that would fill my curse jar with cash. (Yes, I have a curse jar, and my children LOVE to point out words that require deposits. My bonus girl will call me out even on substitute words; I will yell, "Fiddlesticks," and she will call out, "jar." Her point is that the intent is the same, and I'm always talking about how important intent is…tripped up by my own words, again. I told them they can spend the contents of the jar on something decadent when it piles up. If my daughters would just stay in their bedrooms quietly reading and meditating, the jar would remain empty. Back to why I was cursing in acronyms.)

If you have kids, you will run into the problem of the wrong friend or boy/girlfriend. How you handle it differs depending upon the age of your child. When your kids are little, and they bring home a friend who doesn't mesh, you can banish the friend if they don't follow your rules. It might create a short disturbance, but your child will find new friends without too much fuss. As they age, you walk the tightrope of keeping your kids surrounded by people who will support their growth, and forbidding friends who may then look all the more tempting because they are a vehicle for rebellion. When your children reach middle school, the tightrope becomes increasingly thinner.

I started telling my kids in fourth or fifth grade that when it comes to friends who are not on your same level of experience, they can pull you down, or you can pull them up (remember this from Chapter Twelve?). If you are pulling them up, fine. I'm all for helping people who need and want help to better their lives (that's what I do for a living), but as soon as I see that the help is strictly a one-way street or worse, my child is getting sucked dry by an emotional vampire, I go to battle stations. In middle school, battle stations looks like inviting the vampire over and kindly subjecting her to the house rules. If, or when, she doesn't comply, she is sent home. Then we talk about how that friend is pulling my daughter down; I say, "I know how you want to help your friend, but she has to *want* to be helped, and she obviously doesn't."

When it gets to high school, the stakes are much higher. That shaky friend who you could weed out fairly easily in middle school has a tendency to be more sophisticated in their joy-sucking ability by high school. Since teenagers have a tendency toward drama anyway, sometimes it's difficult to tell the difference between regular drama and emotional vampire drama. Emotional vampires specialize in creating drama that keeps them in the center of the swirl. They're seductive at first, because they seem so passionate. Don't confuse passion with drama. Passion moves you forward toward a goal, drama moves you in circles. Drama feeds upon its own energy to keep you in a vortex. It makes you think you're doing something important, but you're not. You're just growing more drama like a virus replicating. Every time you engage in their dramatic story, it changes and mutates, until it eats your time and energy. This is mind candy to the emotional vampire, because now they have company in their story.

Alyssa spent most of her freshman year in her room because she allowed her ambition-sucking "friends" to pull her down. Her grades would drop, I would ground her. She would study, because we took away anything entertaining, and her grades would recover. I would let her off grounding, and the cycle would repeat itself. I prefer grounding as a form of punishment in high school, because it feels good to my Body Compass, but it's not easy on you as a parent. You have to look at their sullen faces every day, because they are home with you instead of out with their friends. Even though it's difficult, I don't give in, because discipline is part of my parenting plan; every time I do something on plan, even if they don't like it, it builds my kids' respect for me.

Back to Alyssa and her broken boy: after years of being grounded on and off in high school, Alyssa was finally a high school graduate, heading off to college on an academic scholarship, and she was legally an adult. And, yet, she was still fascinated with emotional vampires, drawn to their need like a moth to a flame. What could I do except be honest with her? I chose not to ground her anymore, because part of her journey is making mistakes… and it seems a little silly to ground an eighteen-year-old. I could only tell her how she will never be able to fix this boy. I told her that I love her, and I didn't want her to go to his house because of its location. I appealed to her mother hen instinct by asking her if she would let her sister go to that part of town, and then implored her to use the same care with her own precious self. I knew in my heart that the worst thing I could do is to forbid her to see him; that would only increase his bad-boy allure. One thing I knew for sure: I refused to stay quiet. I told the ugly truth: that this boy would eat her light—a light so special that she could shine it upon the world in a way that would make it infinitely more beautiful. I said that she only had so much energy to shine her precious light; if she used it all up on this broken boy, she would have nothing left for herself and the future that shimmers just beyond her sight. But first, I did my own thought work on the situation, so that I went into the conversation clean. I knew that this was all I could do; that's all any parent of a young adult can do. I have raised her for eighteen years to be a smart, kind, loving person with a sense of responsibility to leave this world better than when she arrived. If she takes that charge and spends it on boy after broken boy, that is not my business. All I can do is love her and support her in her good decisions…and pray.

After I did my own thought work on why this boy bothered me so much (I discovered that I thought her choice reflected badly on me…ewww that felt awful, and it wasn't true), I developed some much-needed clarity (this happens every time I do thought work). When I stepped back and looked at the situation without the ego-based fear of how it reflected on me, I realized that her playing savior wasn't fair to *him* in the long run. Then, I sat my daughter down for a talk. I was very honest with her and told her my opinion of the situation. I told her I didn't want her going into his shaky world, especially at night. I said she could bring him into her world, but not the other way around. Then we talked about why she was with someone who obviously didn't fit in her world. I told her that she would never fix this boy; he was too lost and she wasn't a licensed therapist. And if she never intended to stay with him longer than the summer, it would be kinder to break up with him now, before he fell any harder for her. I didn't get mad. I didn't make ultimatums. I just calmly told her my truth. After a copious amount of tears, she saw the truth for what it was. She broke it off with him, not because I said so…but because it was the right thing to do. It was such an amazing lesson in the power of telling the truth, even when the truth is painful. Telling the truth is much easier said than done. It's like other versions of doing the right thing; it's simple, but it's not easy. The beauty part is that your teen will respect you for doing it. Even if they don't like it, they will respect you for it. The more you practice telling your truth, the more your respect balance will increase, not only with your teen, but also with yourself.

If your teen brings home a friend who isn't as fractured as my daughter's broken boy, and yet, you can see that this person is not a good fit, sometimes the best strategy is to wait to see what develops. If you're concerned at all, you want them to "play" at your house, where you control the environment. This goes back to making your home fun-filled, so it's a logical choice to come to your house. Then just hang back and see how it goes. If you're wary, make sure your teen knows that there's an open-door policy until the friend proves worthy; the door remains open, both literally and figuratively. Trust your instincts; if you feel there's something hinky about a new kid, trust that feeling.

If we all trusted our instincts, especially when they go against the Inner Judge's desire to blend in, then the world would be a lot safer. If you have a trouble trusting your instincts, I highly recommend the book *The Gift of Fear* by Gavin de Becker. De Becker is a high-profile security consultant, and his book is one long lesson in trusting the instincts born of thousands of years of survival. When you, or your child, are in unfamiliar territory, that's the time to listen to all those lizard thoughts of survival. Until you can prove them wrong, these thoughts could at the very least save you time misspent on the wrong person, and they might just save your life. One scene in De Becker's book is about a young woman who was walking onto the elevator in her apartment building. There was an attractive young man already on the elevator, and she had a bad feeling about being trapped in a metal box with him. She ignored the feeling and accepted his offer for help with her groceries. Long story short, he attacked her after forcing her into her apartment. If she hadn't followed her instincts to escape when his attention was diverted, she may not have survived to tell the tale, as it was later discovered that he had killed his last two victims. This is a long, drawn out way to say that if you have an instinct about one of your teen's friends, listen and act upon it. You can always repair the relationship *after* you make sure your child is safe.

The dangerous habits of an emotional vampire include using fear and shame as motivating factors. They will convince your kids that if they want to be cool, fit in, or not be lame, then they will do just as the vampire says. The vampire preys on the universal teen desire to blend. I've talked before about the origins of this desire to fit in, but it seems that high school is the most brutal form of campfire; kids believe that if you're outside the circle, your high school experience will suck. The vampire knows this and tempts your teen with a way to be in the center of the circle, except the vampire's way only feeds himself, while sucking the joy and purpose from your child. If you can talk with your teens about how ineffective it is to make decisions out of fear and shame, you may loosen the grip of the vampire. Share with them that decisions made from fear are often bad decisions with dangerous results, just because you are not using your whole brain.

Fear calls up that fight-or-flight response, which shortens your focus to what's right in front of you. When you're in fight or flight, it's impossible to see the possible ramifications down the road... all you can think about is defending yourself or fleeing. And if the emotional vampire is giving you only his or her direction to flee toward, there's no telling where that will lead. They have thought about it, but your kid hasn't. Teach your teen that decisions based in fear, except in emergency situations like jumping out of the way of a runaway car, will void the best of intentions. Because those decisions are only using the part of your brain that speaks lack and attack, there's no higher function use of love and connection. Decisions based in love and connection will lead to a happier more meaningful life, filled with people who love and support you. The more you and your child focus on these kinds of goals, the less attractive either of you will be to an emotional vampire. Also, teach your kids to trust their own instincts about people who seem too good to be true. The emotional vampire that starts out as a fun, super interesting, free spirit may just be an instigator of drama to remain the center of attention...a favorite form of entertainment for E.V.'s. Emotional vampires create problems to solve, so that they don't ever have to grow or develop.

My eldest had a friend that we knew might be trouble, starting in preschool. She was a brilliant kid from a great family, but I knew from the start that something was awry. She didn't value the same things we did as a family, and she was mired in drama from first grade forward. Because I adored her mom, I allowed the relationship to continue long after I should have put a stop to it. She was a big part of why my daughter's freshman year was so awful. When I finally pulled my kid out of the environment that I couldn't control, it took a long time to build our relationship back; that's what can happen if you let a vampire pull your kid into their world. I'm not saying that emotional vampires are all evil; I'm just saying an E.V. will distract your child from her true purpose, in order to have company in their dysfunctional world. As a parent, if you see the situation going down a road that runs off a cliff, it's your duty to put up a roadblock. I believe that you do whatever is necessary to protect your child when they need protecting. In my case, it was necessary to cut off all ties with a kid who had great potential but turned that potential in a direction that ate her future; I wasn't about to let her eat my kid's future as well.

When it comes to your kid's friends, remember, as long as they are under your roof, they play by your rules. You get to make and enforce the rules. Choose wisely which rules you keep as they get into high school; again, if you base the rules about friends on the same value and belief-driven plane as your other rules, you will feel good about enforcing them. Your kids don't have to like the rules, or you, in the short term. That's okay; you have the long view that they can't see yet. Heavy is the head that wears the crown. If you just keep moving in the direction dictated by your values and beliefs, then one day adolescence will be over; and your teen will be an adult who passes on your values and beliefs to his or her own circle of friends. Speaking of growing up, there's no subject that is more fraught with future implications than sex. So I guess it's about time we have that talk.

CHAPTER NINETEEN

The Dreaded Sex Talk
and Other Cautionary Tales

So what do you do when your little ones grow up and start to have more adult distractions, like sex, drugs, and alcohol? The series of television ads that focused on parents as the anti-drug was right on target. If you're involved in your child's life and you ask those tough questions, he will tell you what's going on or, at least, the most important part of what's going on. He may not want to tell you at first but, as a parent, it's your duty to keep asking until he does. More than anything, this tenacity shows them that you care, and his welfare is more important to you than the uneasy tranquility that comes from not asking tough questions. That kind of tranquility is only the calm before the storm. If you don't ask questions and stay involved with your pre-teen's life, you will be outside the loop when he becomes a teenager. You won't have any connection established to be an anchor for your teenagers when they need help and guidance. If that connection is not established early, they will turn elsewhere for advice. They may tell their friends, "My mom's such a drag. She is so overprotective." But inside, they know you care.

Every day in school, your children see kids whose parents don't have rules and who don't care where their kids are or what they're doing. Those are the parents who don't see the importance of being unpopular with their kids, when that's what it takes to nudge them in the right direction. *Parenting is more than caretaking; it's courage in action.* Inside, your kids know that it's better to have a parent who loves them enough to *want* to know what they're doing and thinking, even when what they're doing could make said parent's hair curl—which leads us to the toughest subject of all: sex.

In my experience, the subject of sex polarizes people. Some people are uncomfortable talking about sex (some are made squeamish even thinking about it), and there are others whose every waking thought revolves around sex (these are usually male, but I'm not one to judge). No matter where on this spectrum you fall, talking to your child about sex is never easy. I know when I started thinking about "giving the sex talk" to my eldest daughter, I was immensely uncomfortable. I recalled the story of the romance fiction writer who described her method of writing sex scenes. She was so hesitant about writing the passionate scenes in her novels that she would write around them, and then go back and write them all in one sitting, after a few glasses of wine. That's the only way she could do it, and she made her living talking about sex!

How do you present this difficult subject to your teenager? Better yet, your pre-teen, which is the age when you need to start talking to your child about sex in today's society. The best scenario occurs when your child starts asking questions. It's much easier to move along a conversation that has been started by your child. This conversation may start when your child is quite young, with the question, "Where do babies come from?" I highly recommend not saying, "The stork brings them"; instead, have a version ready that is simple enough for your child to understand and for you to get through without having a heart attack. This excerpt is from an article in *Parent's Magazine* that presents a simple solution which is very close to what I used with my kids when they were little:[32]

"You need to reassure children that they can always ask you a delicate question and get a sensitive and honest answer," says Justin Richardson, MD, coauthor of *Everything You Never Wanted Your Kids to Know About Sex (But Were Afraid They'd Ask)*. This way, your child will be more likely to come to you later in life when sex conversations have broader implications. Look on the internet for versions of ways to talk to your kids about sex, so that you have a simple explanation handy. Always use correct terminology when you are describing body parts, and keep it very simple.

In keeping with my desire to laugh at things that are uncomfortable, here's a funny story: A parent was explaining where babies come from to her eight-year-old son. After a very clinical description of the act, the parent asked, "Okay, honey, do you have any questions?" To which the boy replied, "You don't do that in public, do you?"

If you think it's difficult in elementary school, the ante is even higher when talking to your middle schooler. Even though it is painful to explain a subject to your child that you may feel squeamish about, it will be even more painful if you don't. If you don't talk to your kids about sex, they will go somewhere else to find answers to their questions. You do not want your child to go to their friends for advice on sexual matters. Sex is an adult subject, and you need to convey that to your child. My youngest and I had our last talk about sex after it was discussed in health

---

32 "How to Talk to Your Preschooler About Sex" by Lauren Picker.

class when she was in middle school. That was a great time to talk about it, because it was already on her mind. It didn't seem as awkward when I asked how the teacher presented it in class. We talked about the responses from the other girls in her class. Then I asked her if anyone she knew was sexually active, to which she replied, "Gosh no, Mom, we're only thirteen!" I told her that there were thirteen-year-olds that were sexually active, and it made me so sad that their childhood was cut short like that. She was floored that kids were having sex that young, and that led to an even better discussion about how teenage pregnancy forever changes the life of the teen mom. It wasn't like the stupid shows you see on television. It wasn't dramatic and edgy; it was just sad.

So, if your pre-teen doesn't bring it up, how do you go about initiating the sex talk? First of all, you need to be honest with yourself. You cannot preach something to your child that you don't really believe. You cannot tell your child that it's not okay to have sex before marriage, unless you truly believe that; kids have a way of smelling a lie or an omission. If they catch you in a lie, they will dismiss the rest of what you have to say, no matter how important it is. That doesn't mean you have to tell them everything you've done in your sexual history; you don't want to send them straight to the therapist's couch! You just need to be honest. I told my daughter that when I was in college, I slept with some guys that I really wished I hadn't, and I did it for all the wrong reasons. I traded sex for what I thought was intimacy, and I ended up very disappointed in myself. You need to tell your kids that sex is not a bad thing; in fact, it's so good that it will mess with their head. That's all the more reason to wait until you are old enough to handle the emotions that go along with it.

Secondly, try to not be embarrassed when talking with your child or you will subliminally convey that sex is embarrassing. You need them to know that sex is nothing to be squeamish about, and there's no real mystery to the act. You definitely do not want your daughter or son to be too embarrassed to talk to their potential partner or use a condom to protect themselves. You want to convey that sex is NOT what they see on TV, in the movies, or what they hear their favorite artist rap about on iTunes. It's not some animalistic workout without consequences or attachments. It's also not something that needs to be done with every person who catches their eye. Sex is something very special that is shared between two people who love each other. I tell my girls that your body and your heart are gifts; think very carefully about whom you will bestow those gifts upon.

Unless your religion teaches otherwise, you don't have to be married before you have sex, but you do have to be sure. I tell my girls, "You must be sure that you love this person, you are committed to them, and they are committed to you as well. You also have to be smart. You must choose a form of birth control, and your partner needs to be part of the birth control decision. If you can't talk to your partner about birth control, then you're not ready to have sex with them. You also need to think about HIV tests before the act is consummated. You are not just having sex with your partner; you are having sex with your partner's whole sexual history." One mother I know told her daughter that her potential boyfriend might be "to die for," but she needn't put that to the test. Young people think they're invincible, but a sexually transmitted disease will put a real chink in their invincibility armor. As a parent, you want to equip them with the tools to protect themselves before they have sex.

This is an excerpt from a blog post that I published on my teen blog, GirlTalk[33]. This conveys the tone that has been most successful for me when talking to teenagers about sex. I hope it will spark some discussion in your household:

You think that your parents are so out of touch, but they too were horny teenagers back when dinosaurs roamed the earth. In the seventies and eighties, everybody was sleeping around; we just didn't talk about it. Now, everybody talks about it, and sings about it, and makes videos about it. America is the most hypocritical nation when it comes to sex. Advertisers use sex to sell everything from cars to mascara, and yet if an actress happens to show too much skin, she's publicly flogged. So how much is too much?

Let's first look at why the subject of sex comes up: is it because it's spring and that guy in chemistry class is hot enough to light your Bunsen burner without a match? Or is it because you've been dating someone you love for months, and the time has come to take it to the next level? The first scenario is not a valid reason to drop your drawers; that's the kind of sex that's followed by regrets and the walk of shame. The second scenario is much less likely to make you regret your decision, provided you are using protection, and you're *really* sure. Sex is not a pair of shoes you can send back to Zappos because they didn't fit. There is no free return postage on this decision; once you've lost your virginity, it's gone. Sex can be the best and most fun way to show someone you love them, or it can be the most demeaning act imaginable. It's all in the motivation. Sex doesn't have to be the animalistic

---

33 girltalkteens.tumblr.com/

bump and grind you see in music videos. Just because a guy is a dog, doesn't mean you have to support his behavior. We are not animals; we do not lick our privates in public or turn around three times before we lie down!

How will guys know how to treat girls unless we train them? Just because the media portrays women as needing to dress and act like a porn star to get a guy, doesn't mean it's true. Guys think that they are in charge; they aren't. Girls hold all the power when it comes to sex; a guy cannot make you do anything if you don't want to do it. If you are afraid to say "no," that is a much bigger problem. When he says, "If you loved me, you'd show me," he's lying. If a guy makes you think you have to have sex when you don't want to, that's an act of violence and intimidation, not love…and if you feel intimidated, run. If you are uncomfortable talking about sex with a guy, you definitely should not go any further than talk.

Sex can and should be about love. Your body is a gift; make sure the person you give it to is someone you cherish and someone you will remember with a smile when, and if, you move on.

Did you notice that I didn't say, "Don't have sex, no matter what." That just makes it more appealing as an avenue of rebellion. Rebellion is the extreme form of independence; you want your teens to become independent, not rebellious. If you don't give them hard and fast rules to fight against, then rebellion doesn't come up. If you let your teen know that her actions are her own, and you realize that having sex is ultimately her and her partner's decision, then you are treating them like the adults they think they are. I do not condone teen sex; I think it's too much power too soon. But I'm also not naïve enough to think that my kids would refrain from sex just because I said so. However, if I can have a frank discussion with them and treat them like adults, they might just listen to a rationale that is introduced in a manner that refers to sex in a way that is closer to what's actually happening in high school. I have read things on teen sites that would shock you—parties where boys and girls are demeaning each other in a way that literally makes me sick. The way to stop this is not to preach to teens about how awful sex is; do you remember how hormonal you were in high school?

You can't forget that you were young once; if you do, you will pay the price. When your kids are little, it's fun to remember what it was like to be a kid; when they're older, it's imperative. I see parents all the time who seem to have been born fully formed with a receding hairline and a paunch. They forget that they too had trouble sitting still in church when they were less than three feet tall or how lame they thought their parents' ideas were when they were teenagers. This attitude does their kids a great injustice. Two positive results will come from remembering your childhood: 1) you have more empathy for your child, and 2) your child will respect your opinion more. When you start to see things from your kids' point of view, it means the world to them. When their best friend is mad at them, or they got a C on a test they thought they nailed, it's trivial to us. But if you put yourself back into their situation, you can remember how devastating these things are for them. If you communicate with your teens on their level, your status will rise exponentially in their eyes. The greatest gift you can give your kids' is to let him know that you understand what he's feeling and that you care about his pain. That doesn't mean you have to fix it for him every time; sometimes the best action you can take is to just listen (I've found this goes double for spouses).

When your children understand that you remember being a kid, they know that you probably also remember manipulating your parents. They won't even try half the things their friends do with their parents, just because they know you're too savvy. You have instantly depleted their arsenal of kid weapons just by thinking like a kid yourself…and you were doing it to be caring; what a bonus! When your kids know that you think on their level, and they can't fool you, it builds your respect bank account. The most effective kind of parenting continually makes deposits into that account: whether it's by thinking like a kid, thereby staying on a level plane of understanding with your child, or by being consistent in discipline and not giving in when the going gets tough.

When that respect account balance grows, the problems with your child's behavior will diminish proportionately. There is never a 100 percent certainty that your children will do what you tell them to do when they are away from you, but if they respect you *and* your decisions, the likelihood increases dramatically. If they hold your beliefs and values in high esteem, they will be more apt to follow your guidelines automatically when the appropriate situation arises. They will adopt your opinions as their own; they will turn down that joint or that drink because they know it's the right thing to do, not just because it's your rule.

I had a brilliant demonstration of this last weekend. My daughter was driving us to the football game a couple of hours away while I read. She got a text, and I asked her if she wanted me to read it to her; this was necessary BECAUSE WE DON'T TEXT AND DRIVE! She said, "Sure." It was a text from the bonus child to all their friends about game day. She was offering to meet up with them after the game, and she typed, "If you guys need any help, Alyssa and I will be sober." My girls are all mother-hen types. I'm not saying they never drink; they *are* in college. I do know that they comment negatively about when other girls get drunk, sloppy, and sleep with guys they would never look at twice if they were sober. This is all I could hope for when I sat them down and talked with them about the costs of sex, drugs, and alcohol. The problem with all three is not that they are inherently bad; the problem arises when you use them to excess as a way to escape your life. If you need sex, drugs, and alcohol to escape your life, your life is the problem. If you can teach your kids that using sex, drugs, or alcohol to escape their life is a choice, then you empower them to say no. That doesn't mean that I don't say, "No sex, no drugs, and no drinking and driving" when they go out on weekends, because I do…every time they leave the house. But I do it more as a touchstone, so that they think about saying, "We know, Mom. No sex, no drugs, no drinking and driving" as they leave my circle of influence.

When your kids are juniors or seniors in high school, your influence is tangential at best. They have already decided who they are as people, all you can do is tell them that you trust them and believe in them, and then be there as a sounding board if they get in trouble. Trust that your parenting plan has done its job, and you have delivered a thoughtful kid who represents your family values. And now let's look at how you create your own plan.

CHAPTER TWENTY

Crafting Your Own Parenting Plan

I have spent many pages outlining parts of my parenting plan for you, because I know it works. But your plan may not look exactly like mine, and that's okay. Your plan is based upon a long-term view of the adult your kid will become someday. What do you want that adult to act like; what values and beliefs do you want them to have? What do you want that child to thank you for when she reaches adulthood and starts having her own children? Figure that out, and then work backward to write your plan. It's kind of like using the flow chart from Chapter Twelve, with the desired task being the development of a kind, caring, accomplished adult. If you follow your parenting plan no matter what your kids throw at you, I'm speaking figuratively of course, it will work. The empowerment and self-respect that comes from successful parenting is the Holy Grail that you thought you were searching for in a successful career. You can have a successful career as well, but just know that you may have to wait until your kids are older and in need of less care to do it. It will be worth the wait; I promise!

So what elements of my parenting plan do I feel are most important? Let me detail the Top 10 Hits:

Spend Time with Your Kids: Since we all have a choice in how we spend our time, I highly recommend choosing to spend time with your kids as much as possible. You will never regret spending more time with your kids when you're sitting in that rocking chair at age eighty-five, reflecting upon your life. My husband was my mentor for this concept. Back when Hurricane Ivan hit the Gulf Coast, he was sought after by a big contracting firm out of Atlanta. He had a good reputation as a builder (because he's a great guy and a competent and honorable builder), and when the firm asked around about someone who could handle a big job reliably, his name naturally came up. There was a ton of rebuilding to be done after this devastating storm, and this company was willing to pay big bucks for a local supervisor. They offered him $1,000 per day for six months; the caveat was that he would be working seven days a week without time off. His first reaction was "no," but he told the guy he would have to talk to his wife. When he told me the offer, my first reaction was, "$180,000 in six months, are you kidding? How can we make this work?" He just smiled at me and said, "We can't. Our baby is two years old. There is no amount of money that would make me miss six months of watching her grow." And that's why I married him. His priorities are crystal clear.

Respect for Self: Self-respect includes a practice of self-care. Put on your own oxygen mask first. This looks different for different people, but some form of quiet reflection, whether it be meditation or a daily walk, is something you can do for yourself without spending any money or much time. Meditation and exercise will make you a better parent and a better person in general. The satisfaction you gain from meditation and exercise is better than shoes and chocolate combined...that's as good as it gets in my book! Honoring your own needs will teach your kids to do the same. There's no substitute for leading by example. Respect your own gifts; just because it comes easily to you doesn't mean it's not valuable. Teach your kids to do the same.

Respect for Others: Celebrate the artist in everyone. Until you can appreciate that everyone is special for their own unique talents, you won't be able to pursue your own. Don't expect others to approve of your path to pursue your unique talents, especially if it requires change. It may be time to pursue what makes you joyful in spite of what everybody thinks; then, and only then, will "your" people find you. If the people who surround you don't support your dreams, they are not "your" people. Wish them well and keep searching for "your" people. Your people don't have to live next door; I have many supportive friends who are far away from me, but we keep in touch via the internet and telephone. When I'm feeling lost or down, I have a handful of people I can call or write who will bolster me; all I have to do is ask. Teach your children to surround themselves with friends who they respect and who also respect them, just the way they are. That way, they will have a support system to rely on when the going gets tough.

Responsibility for Your Actions: Tell the truth and apologize when you mess up. Teach your kids the power of the ability to fail without making a big deal about it. Failure is the best learning tool there is; Thomas Edison said, "If I find 10,000 ways something won't work, I haven't failed. I am not discouraged, because every wrong attempt discarded is often a step forward."[34] Failure is all in

---

34 www.thomasedison.com/quotes.html

perception; it took me sixteen years to write this book. Each time I thought it was crap and put it away, it was a failure to write that book. Thank goodness I didn't succeed with those other books, because this is the one I was supposed to finish. Remember, *you're exactly where you're supposed to be to learn the lesson you're supposed to learn.* Taking responsibility for your thoughts is as important as taking responsibility for your actions; use Thought Work to clean up energy-draining crappy thoughts, and then teach your children to do the same.

Rules Are Good; Consistent Rules Are Better: Develop rules and a system of discipline that are appropriate for the age of your child and are consistently applied. Consistent rules give your kids a foundation to grow from. They also instill a force field that your children can use as a shield when other kids ask them to do something that goes against your rules. As your kids age, pare your rules down to only a few that reflect your family values.

Family Values Create a Happy Home: Come up with a list of traits and characteristics of the perfect friend or mate, and then work backward to figure out what values and beliefs those traits have in common. Whether that means you travel to see how other cultures live, craft instead of watch TV, or practice random acts of kindness, establish your values; then come up with traditions that reflect those values…and stick to those traditions. Don't forget to hug your kids every time they walk by. This will lead to a fun atmosphere that will make your home the place that all the kids want to visit, which means you keep your kids within your sphere of influence as they develop the independence that will serve them when they leave you.

Ride the Change Cycle, and Teach Your Children to Do the Same: When things go to hell in a hand basket, remember that it's just Square One again. Sometimes the Square One struggle is initiated by emotional vampires trying to suck all the joy and light from your kid. Don't be afraid to fight for your kids; their safety and welfare is more important than rocking the boat. A rocky boat is better than a lost kid. Don't rush Square Two, be courageous in Square Three and practice self-care to keep your energy level up, and enjoy Square Four because, before you know it, you'll be back to Square One again.

Work Your Own Thoughts before You Confront Your Child: If you are under the false impression that your way is the only right way, you are falling into a thought trap. If you think that you're the only person who can do anything for your children, then you're setting yourself up for migraines, TMJ, acid reflux, and a host of other stress-related diseases. If you think you have to suffer to be a good parent, I am here to tell you, "That's a crock." They don't give out points for suffering in Heaven; I'm pretty sure that suffering is on the schedule of a more southerly celestial destination. The only use for suffering that I have found is that it's a quick and dirty way to get pity points. The question is, "Are pity points worth all the negative energy that self-induced suffering creates?" There's no joy in pity; at the end of the day, pity makes everyone feel, well, pitiful. So clean up your own thoughts, and teach your kids to do the same. If a thought causes you suffering, it's based upon a falsehood. The truth may hurt sometimes, but it doesn't cause lasting suffering like a crappy thought trap does.

Listen to Your Teen Twice as Much as You Talk to Them: This math is simple to understand, but difficult to apply. If you can understand the difference between talking *with* your teen and talking *at* your teen, the equation becomes clearer. If the reason you're having a conversation starts with a feeling of righteous indignation or you need to "sit them down and show them where they're wrong, dammit," you can bet you're about to talk "at" them. If this is the foundation for your conversation, you might as well save your breath. Take the energy you would have put into that confrontation and go do your own thought work first. When you've figured out why you're so mad, and where you are manifesting that behavior in your own life, *then* you can have a chat with your teens. Use "I" words when you talk, and then ask for their reaction; when they begin to talk, keep your mouth shut until they're done (this is hard…sometimes near impossible). No matter how ridiculous you think their reasoning is, it's important to them for you to listen to it in full. That way you build that respect bank account that will see both of you through the rough times.

Stay in Your Own Business: When your teen is having an issue at school or with their friends, remember to stay on the sidelines. If your kids feel like they're drowning, you can't help them if you jump in the pool with them. If you stay on the side of the pool, you can easily throw them a life preserver and help both of you successfully. Martha Beck has a concept called "clean pain vs. dirty pain" that is quite helpful with teens. If you hit your thumb with a hammer, your thumb will hurt. The throbbing thumb pain is clean pain. There's a direct relationship between the injury and the resulting pain; this pain will pass. The stories you tell yourself about your throbbing thumb is dirty pain. Like, "Mother of Pearl, my thumb hurts! And now I won't be able to write today! I have a freaking deadline, and I'm never going to make it now that I hurt my freaking thumb. Oh my God, what am I going to do?" At this point, you are so in your head, you may not even notice your thumb. It's the same thing with your teens. If one of their friends is rude to them, that hurt is clean. When she starts spinning stories about what it means about *her* that her friend was rude, then the swirling circles of dirty pain will threaten to drown her. If her friend is rude without cause, then that's not a friend worth having…period. The pain of losing a friend is clean Square One stuff; the stories our kids tell themselves about how they will never have another friend; they will be left by the side of the road, friendless and alone…a social outcast for the rest of their lives: that's dirty pain. See the difference? When you feel as though you're in a dirty-pain prison, make sure you're not the one carrying around your own bars. If you are confused about whether you are in clean pain or wallowing in dirty pain, ask yourself, "Does it feel 'shackles on' or 'shackles off'?" Clean pain will hurt, but it doesn't make you feel shackles on.

These Top 10 are the tools I use most in my day-to-day parenting, but I haven't been using them for my whole parenting career. In the beginning, before my year of deaths and cancer, I still had a parenting plan based upon what I wanted my kids to be like as adults. My family values and beliefs were in place; it was the execution of the plan that was faulty. My kids were still great kids, because I had the plan in place, but I didn't take care of myself and lead by example. My self-talk was 75% critical, 5% complimentary, and 20% gibberish about what other people would say if they saw what I was doing. I was in victim mode most of my waking moments, and that's a very ineffective way of raising your kids; unless you want them to become victims as well. I was caught in the wolf-baby trap.

Since I was raised in an environment where I was always looking for the next threat, I lived my life in fight or flight mode. I knew that I adored my kids, but I didn't know how to care for them from within victim mode. Being constantly on guard leaves little room for nurturing, either for yourself or for your children. Then I found Martha Beck and her life coaching tools, and everything changed. I know the tools work, because they work for me and my clients. Since I've started using them, my relationship with my kids has become immeasurably closer; I might add, that my relationship with myself has become more balanced as well. If you write your plan and use these tools, you can turn things around... like I did.

Take my Top 10, keep what feels right to you, and then toss the rest...I won't mind; hell, I won't even know, unless you tell me. In fact, I would love it if you came up with some of your own and then told me about them. Follow your Body Compass (and Body Dousing and Shackles On/Off) to lead you in the direction of love. Because that's all Plugged-In Parenting comes down to: above all, love your kids. Tell them and show them as much as possible. Do whatever works to bring more love into your parenting. It doesn't matter if it's the latest thing, approved by "everybody"; it only matters that it works. It will never hurt your children to hug them or pick them up when you feel compelled; I don't care what the old aunties say about spoiling a child. You can't spoil them by showing affection. I carried my eldest until I had her sister two years later, and she's the most confident, independent young woman I know. She had two jobs while going to school full-time at NYU, because she wanted to make her own way…and all the old ladies who saw me carrying her as a toddler said I would make her dependent upon me and spoil her rotten. Hah! I thumb my nose at them! If you love your kids and follow your Inner Guide's wisdom without giving a fig what "everybody will think," then you can craft a parenting plan that will lead to confident, successful kids.

It may take you a while to come up with a plan, so go ahead and start now, using baby steps to write it. Set your alarm for ten minutes, or whatever amount of time seems ridiculously easy, and write about what you want your graduating valedictorian (or similarly successful future role) to say about you as a parent when she's on the podium. Then work your way backward in your plan to fill in the necessary elements of an atmosphere that will foster the growth of that young adult. Then fill in your to-do list with action steps you need to take as a parent to make that atmosphere a reality. Then use baby steps to craft a household that delivers that atmosphere, and become that parent.

No matter what happened to you in your childhood, you can recover and become a Plugged-In Parent. Regardless of how awful it was for you as a kid, you can overcome it…because it's not happening to you anymore. The past is in the past. In the words of Alicia Keys, "the present is a gift"; you get to open it every day and use it as you see fit. I know if you were abused or neglected, it's difficult to ever feel normal or whole again. That's what Plugged-In Parenting can do for you. You can heal the child within you.

In the process of nurturing and loving your children, you can nurture and heal your inner child from whatever wounds he or she is still carrying around. That's the best part of parenting. No pill or religion feels better than being a good parent; it's almost as if you can erase the mistakes of your own parents by giving yourself to your kids. You close the karmic circle. As a wolf-baby parent, you have two choices: 1) You can continue to stay closed-off from your kids, blaming your crappy childhood for not being able to open up, or 2) You can develop a meaningful relationship with your children by being vulnerable, thereby healing old scars and making yourself whole again. It's your choice. I wish you all the luck and love in your parenting journey; it may seem a Herculean task at times and lighter than air at others. Both situations are completely normal and exactly as they're supposed to be. John Lennon was credited with saying some memorable quotes, but my favorite is, "Everything will be all right in the end. If it's not all right, it's not yet the end."

Well, this is the end, and it's all right.

About Terri Fedonczak

Terri Fedonczak has 22 years of parenting experience and is a Certified Martha Beck life coach, specializing in parent and teen coaching.

Terri wants to live in a world where girls recognize their own power and choose to use it for good. On a trip to Londolozi Game Reserve in South Africa, she witnessed the power of lionesses, as they supported each other within the pride; it was a lightning bolt of realization, leading her on a mission to bring the Power of the Pride to girls and their parents.

After 16 years as a commercial real estate agent, a bout with breast cancer transformed Terri's life in 2010, making her realize that time with her four girls and patient husband was a much better deal than money and status. It was time to put her mission into action. She left sales and embarked on a journey of spreading the message of Girl Power for Good.

Terri Fedonczak takes the Girl Power message into schools, talking to teen girls about how to thrive in the wilds of high school. When she's not writing books, speaking, coaching or blogging, you can find her paddle boarding on the sparkling waters of Boggy Bayou, knitting to the consternation of her children, who are buried in scarves and hats, or dancing in her kitchen to Motown.

You can discover your own inner lioness and feel the Power of the Pride at www.girlpowerforgood.com.

Index